ON THE ROAD TO FREEDOM

Canadian-East European Relations, 1963-1990

Aloysius Balawyder

East European Monographs, Boulder

Distributed by Columbia University Press, New York

2005

I wish to dedicate this monograph to my parents, Isidore and Katarina.

TABLE OF CONTENTS

PREFACE

This monograph continues the narrative on Canada's relations with Eastern Europe. In my first volume, *In the Clutches of the Kremlin,* I dealt with these relations during the Cold War period whereas in the current volume, *On the Road to Freedom, Canadian-East European Relations, 1963-1991* I relate the manner by which Canada attempted to encourage the nascent forces of indepen-dence and freedom without precipitating crises.

In both monographs I deal with such topics as trade and Canadian foreign policy but in this monograph I also treated such issues as international claims, détente, Helsinki Accords and the gradual demise of the Soviet Empire. In order to provide background information on Eastern Europe I surveyed the history of this region, outlined its geography, demography and industries and show, in some measure, why Canada was interested in having relations with the Soviet-bloc countries.

Canada took an active part in fostering a spirit of good will and co-operation with these countries. She helped to build "confidence," and to "know them better." My interviews of former Canadian diplomats indicate the role Canada played in that part of the world. Her efforts and those of many other countries bore fruit as demonstrated by the signing of the historic Helsinki Accords by thirty-five countries. Canada along with Denmark played an important role in monitoring the observance of human rights issues, an important aspect of the Accords.

During the "détente" there were countless contacts between the peoples, the governments and diplomats from both sides of the "iron curtain." Scientific, academic and cultural exchanges flourished; trade increased and the movement of people in the form of immigration and visits multiplied. The Western world met the Eastern world in a creative way. Some of the barriers of the Cold War began disappearing and were, to some extent, replaced by acceptance and understanding.

Despite the successes of the "détente," there still remained much to be done in the great project of building "bridges" between the two worlds. The invasion of Czechoslovakia by Soviet-led forces in 1968 and the imposition of martial law in

Poland in 1981 were jolts in the era of détente.

The advent of two individuals on the world scene helped the forces of change and progress. One of these individuals was Mikhail Gorbachev who was chosen in 1985 to be the secretary general of the Communist Party of the Soviet Union. Using the two-prong approach; namely "perestroika," and "glasnost," he attempted to bring about badly needed political, economic and cultural reforms in the Soviet Union and in her satellites. Above all, he provided an option to the Soviet republics and to the Soviet-bloc countries by inviting them to either march under the Soviet Union's banner or to strike out on their own independent course.

The other individual was Pope John Paul II. Elected to the highest position in the Catholic Church in 1978, he exerted tremendous influence not only on Catholics in Poland but also on many people in Eastern Europe and throughout the world. People of different languages, creeds and political stripes applauded his insistence on the sacredness of human rights. He encouraged his own people to persevere in their attempts to be free and independent. This message reached other East Europeans giving them also hope and courage in their march to freedom.

This monograph could not have come into the light without the assistance of many generous people. The members of the National Archives of Canada were most co-operative in screening copious documents from the department of External Affairs and other departments and making them available for my research. My wife, Martha, helped me with the index and checked the interviews I had had with the former Canadian diplomats. Kim Sherrington from the Antigonish Computer Centre patiently and competently assisted me in preparing the manuscript for publication. Above all, my colleague, Professors Guy LaLande, a member of the History Department and Professor Thomas Roach, a retired member of the Art Department, both from St. Francis Xavier University, provided yeoman's service by correcting my typos, improving the grammatical structure of sentences and correcting factual errors. Special thanks to Professor Paul Robert Magocsi for permitting me to use his *Historical Atlas of Central Europe*, (Seattle, Toronto and London), 2002, p.205.

AB

LIST OF TABLES

Central Europe, 1980

I. INTRODUCTION

The term Eastern Europe means different things to different people. Many consider the term to mean the six countries under study in this monograph: Poland, Czechoslovakia, Yugoslavia, Hungary, Romania and Bulgaria. Others would divide this territory into Central Europe consisting of Poland, Czechoslovakia and Hungary and the Balkans made up of Yugoslavia, Romania and Bulgaria.[1] In the post World War years (1945-1990) these countries were generally called satellites or communist states. To many English- and French-speaking Canadians these countries were faraway places inhabited by people who spoke incomprehensible languages, wore strange looking clothes and practiced curious customs during Easter and Christmas time, and relished certain types of food.

Unlike Germany, France and England East European countries were subsumed as parts of four empires: German, Russian, Austrian and Ottoman.[2] For the most part they were treated as serfs eking out their livelihood by working on land. They had no country of their own for many centuries. Poles were fortunate to be given in 1807 a territory called the Grand Duchy of Warsaw by Napoleon Bonaparte as a reward for the Polish contribution in the Napoleonic wars. The Congress of Vienna 1814-1815 enlarged this territory and placed it under the jurisdiction of the czar of Russia. Two other countries received recognition in the 19th century, namely Hungary in 1867 when she joined Austria to form a dual monarchy and Bulgaria who received her independence from the Ottoman Empire in 1878-79.

Three new and independent countries, Poland, Czechoslovakia and Yugoslavia were created after World War I and received official recognition by the framers of the Peace Treaties of 1919-1920. These successor states soon discovered that gaining independence was one thing; the organization of successful democratic governments was something different. Proliferation of political parties, mismanagement and intrigue shattered the dreams of many people.

These dreams became nightmares when Europe was overrun by Nazi Germany and later became a victim of the Soviet Union. At the Yalta Conference in 1945, Winston Churchill, the prime minister of Great Britain and

Franklin Roosevelt, the president of the United States, succumbed to the demands of Stalin allowing him to make Eastern Europe a buffer against a possible attack by Germany. In turn he promised that each of the East European states would have "free and unfettered elections." That did not happen. Instead, assisted by the KGB and the Red Army, communist governments were installed in all of these countries. The general pattern of the imposed Soviet manipulation consisted of three steps; controlled elections, pseudo-coalition and complete communist takeover.

Canadian Intellectuals assess Eastern Europe

Most Canadians had a sketchy knowledge of the peoples from Eastern Europe, meeting them in the work place, in shopping malls, in churches, at meetings, in recreation places. During World War II Canadians followed the events that transpired in Europe and became acquainted with the names of Russian and East European towns and cities that were being bombed. The presence of veterans from the Second World War and the Korean War reminded Canadians that they were citizens of the world and the interests, struggles and challenges of other peoples became somehow their own struggles and challenges.

Some of Canadian academics and politicians did not have much interest in Eastern Europe. Prior to 1960 most Canadian universities had courses on Russian and Soviet history, political science and economics; but precious little on Eastern Europe. There were comparatively few books and periodicals in the university libraries on Eastern Europe. Some academics did not consider this part of the world significant enough to hire specialists in these fields nor to reallocate funds from the study of Canadian, West European and American areas to East European studies.

A change began to appear. In 1954 the Canadian Association of Slavists, (CAS) was formed and a journal, *Canadian Slavonic Papers*, launched. The Canadian International Service of the C.B.C (CIS-CBC) began to transmit news and commentaries to Eastern Europe in Czech, Slovak, Russian, Ukrainian and Polish languages.[3] The purpose of this service was to inform the citizens of these countries what Canadians were doing and to underline the quality of life they were enjoying.

In 1966 CAS decided to have a forum to discuss the place of Eastern Europe in Canadian foreign policy. Professor Gordon Skilling from the Political Economy Department, at the University of Toronto presented a discussion paper entitled "Canada and Eastern Europe."[4] He pointed out that Canada's diplomatic relations with the Soviet Union began in 1943, with Czechoslovakia and Poland in 1947 and with Yugoslavia in 1948. He indicated how relations with Eastern Europe were important in the light of Canada's need for trade, cultural, academic and scientific exchanges and for her continuous search for peace and security.[5] In his opinion the East European Canadian community made these relations significant, even though East Europeans comprised but five percent of the total Canadian population.

Senator Stanley Haidaz confirmed Professor Skilling's observations. He pointed out that the Canadian government was not only satisfied with the existing Canadian legations in Eastern Europe but that Ottawa was shortly planning to open legations in Hungary, Bulgaria and Romania. Statistics show that Canada increased her trade with Eastern Europe by 250 per cent from 1963 to1966. The Canadian government was also eager to increase her scientific, educational and artistic exchanges with Eastern Europe.

However, some of the members of the group felt that less than two percent of Canada's total export-import trade did not justify increased relations with Eastern Europe. In addition, the small increase of cultural and scientific exchanges did not warrant spending added monies that could be required. Rather this money, according to one observer, could be better used in developing the existing legations in other countries[7].

The majority of the members supported Skilling and Haidaz. One participant argued that trade and exchanges have been the chief means of "promoting East-West relations."[8] An expert on foreign policy of Eastern Europe argued that Canada's role lay in building bridges between the East and the West.[9] Having a market for its surplus grain was, according to an economist, another reason for developing stronger ties with the Soviet-bloc countries. Time showed that the majority was correct on most counts.

Canadian foreign policy and Eastern Europe

Canadian foreign policy was and to a large extent continues to be based on Canada's need for international trade; her close relationship with the United States and Great Britain; her membership in the United Nations and in the North Atlantic Treaty Organization; her ethnic East European population and her need for security. Canada's relations with the communist-bloc countries ebbed and flowed with East-West relations. A crisis involving any country of the two alliances affected Canada. For instance, the invasion of

Afghanistan in 1979 by the Soviet Union had repercussions on Canada, who along with NATO countries decided to impose sanctions on the Soviet Union and on the Soviet-bloc states. In 1981 Canada in concert with her allies she also imposed sanctions on Poland when the latter declared martial law.

Canadian foreign policy did change significantly since the Cold War. During the Cold War period the "containment" policy aimed to stem the Soviet aggression in Europe, Asia and Africa was put into effect. With the coming of détente, "confidence building" and "trust replaced "containment." Western powers learned from their helplessness to aid the people in the Hungarian Revolution of 1956 that military force was not the answer to Soviet imperialism. Following the invasion of Czechoslovakia in 1968 both Soviet Union and the Western powers expressed their readiness to co-operate in reducing tensions and solving some of the East-West problems. Early in 1970 both sides began to explore the possibility of a conference on Co-operation and Security in Europe (CSCE). Canada was very pleased to learn of this possibility and looked forward to contribute to this movement in any way she could.

The outcome of the CSCE was the Helsinki Accords. Canada and Denmark played an important role as members who were delegated to monitored human rights infractions. They dutifully reported their findings to the 35 member-states at their periodic conferences. Many of the infractions of human rights occurred in Eastern Europe.

The Helsinki Accords did not focus solely on human rights; the free movement of people, cultural and scientific exchanges were equally important. Under Article 2 of the Accords, trade was encouraged as a means of "building bridges" between the East and West. In the mid-1970 and early 1980s the Soviet Union, Poland and Hungary permitted some of their citizens to travel abroad. Yugoslavia encouraged her citizens to work in Germany and even emigrate under the umbrella of "family reunification".[10]

The East European ethnic composition of Canada had an influence on Canada's foreign policy even though the Slavic group comprised only five percent of the Canadian population. The majority of East European Canadians were rabid anti-communists and from time to time presented briefs to the Canadian government decrying the cruel treatment of their kinsmen and kinswomen in Europe. They cautioned Ottawa about undesirable prospective immigrants and at the same time lobbied the Government to widen the immigration regulations in order to permit more of their friends and relatives to enter Canada. As Canadians, East Europeans contributed significantly to arts, science, education and music. Many of them fought as Canadians in the armed forces and gave their lives for their country of their birth or adoption. Although many observed the customs and traditions of their parents and grandparents, they professed their loyalty to Canada and for what it stood.

Canadian Ethnic Groups

Ethnic Group	1961	1971	1981	1991
Bulgarians	*Statistics are not available*			
Canadians	18,238,200	21,568,300	24,003,495	28,031,000
Czechoslovaks	73,100	81,900	67.695	59,125
Hungarians	126,200	136,900	116.390	100,725
Poles	323,500	314,400	254.480	272,810
Romanians	43,800	27,400	22,495	28,650
Yugoslavs	68,600	105,000	114.595	113,935

Based on *Statistics Canada 1961-1991*

As the table indicates the largest East European groups in Canada were the Poles; the second largest were the Hungarians; third, were the Yugoslavs followed by Czechoslovaks. Although not very numerous, East Europeans encouraged artistic, musical and cultural exchanges between Canada and Soviet bloc countries.

Profile of Eastern Europe

The growing relations between Canada and Eastern Europe can be considered in the light of the large differences in the area size of Canada and Eastern Europe and in the population of these geographical areas. The total area of Canada is 9,976,140 km^2 whereas that of the six Eastern European countries is 1,008,537 km2.[11] Population wise the six East European countries had a population of 116, 806,000 (1990) and Canada had a population of 26, 620, 000 in 1990 which was about 20 per cent of total population of the six Eastern European countries under study.

To have a better understanding of Eastern Europe it is helpful to carry out a brief demographic, economic and historical survey of these countries. The countries are ranked according to population and not necessarily according to their geographical area. Industries and employment will be summarized in order to give the reader information as to what types of products were available for trade. In each case the early history sketch covers the period up to the communist take over. Throughout this volume the other time frames of communist regimes are treated.

"A"

Poland is the largest of the East European countries both in size and in population covering an area of 326,680 km and having a population of 38,112,000 (1990). Its population is homogenous with less than 5% belonging to minority groups. It is bounded on the north by the Baltic Sea; on the northeast and east by the Soviet Union; on the south by Czechoslovakia and on the west by Germany. Although Warsaw, the capital city, suffered a horrendous destruction during the Second World War, it was remarkably rebuilt. Other cities are: the ancient and beautiful city of Cracow; the textile city of Lodz; the industrial cities of Breslau and Poznan and the seaport cities of Gdansk and Szczecin. Before the War Poland was predominantly an agricultural country. With the coming of the communists it became industrialized. However, farming continued to be one of the main occupations of the people who grew such cereals as rye, wheat, oats, flax and such vegetables as sugar beets, cabbage, beans, and onions. Poland also produced some fruits and raised cattle, horses and pigs. Coal mining, fishing, manufacturing and the textile industry were other important occupations.

It is rather an old country dating back to 960 A.D. In 1368 it joined with Lithuania forming one of the largest countries at that time, called the Polish-Lithuanian Commonwealth.[12] It developed an odd type of government whereby not only the Polish magnates but also foreign powers participated, from time to time, in the election of the king. Weakened by internal strife, the elected monarchy and ambitious neighbours it was partitioned three times and remained occupied until 1918.

Her inter-war years were not easy as she struggled economically and politically to become a self-sufficient nation. In 1939 Hitler and the Soviet Union occupied Poland. Poles, however, did not give up the struggle for their independence. Many of them fought along side the allies in the Battle of the

Atlantic, the Battle of Britain, in Africa, Italy and France. The Polish First Armoured Division was part of the Canadian First Army.

But unfortunately after her heroic struggle for independence the communists under the blessing of Moscow-enslaved Poland. The allies including Canada recognized her Provisional Government of National Unity. It was short-lived. In the 1947 elections marred by corruption, coercion and violence, any hope for a free and independent Poland was shattered. Canada was disappointed by the evens but, nevertheless to continue her diplomatic relations initiated during World War II Canada opened a legation in Warsaw in 1947. (See map of East Central Europe.)

"B"

The second largest East European country was Romania with a population of 23,191,000 (1990) and having an area of 237,500km2. On the north and northeast Romania is bounded by Russia; on the east by the Black Sea; on the south by Bulgaria; on the southwest by Yugoslavia and on the northwest by Hungary. The largest and the capital city is Bucharest. Other cities are Cluj, Timosoara and Brasov. The Danubian plain has very fertile black soil where cereals and fruits are grown. Besides agriculture, Romania is noted for its petroleum and natural gas. In addition, some small industries such as metal work, leather tanning, and furniture making reminds visitors of Romanians' expertise in crafts.

The origin of Romania dates back to the Romans who occupied some of the territory we know as Romania. In the 19th century Romania came under the control of Turkey. In 1859 the two provinces of Wallachia and Moldavia were united under a prince and eighteen years later Romania threw off the tutelage of Turkey and became independent. In 1918 the disputed provinces of Bessararbia and Transylvania were added to her existing territory.[13]

With the aid of the Red Army communists under the leadership of Petru Groza who used the leftist group, the People's Democratic Front, to take control of the country. The key ministries of interior, justice and defence were taken over by the communists. In 1947 Romania signed a peace treaty with the Western allies including Canada thus officially ending hostilities between Romania and the West. Canada established diplomatic relations with Romania in 1973. (See map.)

"C"

The third largest East European country with whom Canada established diplomatic relations was Yugoslavia, a country created in 1918 having a population of 20,411,000 (1990) and covering an area of 220,327km^2. It borders on seven countries; to the east lie Austria and Hungary; to the east lie Rumania and Bulgaria; to the south, Greece; to the south and west, Albania and to the northwest, Italy. Its largest city and capital is Belgrade. Other large cities are Zagreb, Sarajevo, Ljubljana, Skopje and Novi Sad. It is both an agricultural and an industrial country. Its farm produce consists of potatoes, sugar beets, hops, rice, flax, fruits, tobacco, and fruits. The farmers also raised livestock and poultry. Her exports consist of medicinal plants, fruits, wines, tobacco and lead. Her imports are largely textiles, machinery, electrical appliances and chemicals. From time to time Yugoslavia purchased grain from Canada.

Unlike any other East European country, Yugoslavia a federated state comprised of five "official" nations and a number of minorities.[14] The so-called nations were Serbs, Croats, Slovenes, Macedonians, and Montenegrins and the minorities consisted of Romanians, Hungarians, Bulgarians, Slovaks, Czechs, Italians, Germans and Gypsies.

During the inter-war period this country was called the Kingdom of Serbs, Croats and Slovenes, but in 1927 the name was changed to Yugoslavia, the country of Southern Slavs. Like Poland it faced many political, religious, economic and ethnic problems. During World War II Hitler attempted to conquer it but after bitter battles gave up. The leading opponent of the Germans and a fearless and dedicated communist was Jozef Broz, nicknamed "Tito" because he continually ordered his people to do things.

In 1947 Canada opened a legation in Belgrade and three years later it was raised to the level of an embassy. Canadian Slavic groups criticized the Canadian government for doing so in light of Yugoslavia's record of religious and human rights violations. Most Canadians and particularly Canadian Slavic groups, Roman Catholics and French Canadians were critical of Tito and his regime even after he broke his ties with Stalin in 1949. Tito vowed to lead the country on its own road to "socialism," but was extremely careful not to antagonize the Kremlin. He joined a group of non-aligned countries and kept correct but not necessarily friendly relations with the Soviet Union or her satellites. (See map.)

"D"

The fourth largest East European country with whom Canada established relations was Czechoslovakia, a country of 15,661,000 (1990) covering an area of 97,690 km^2. This wedge-shaped country shares its borders with Germany and Poland on the north; with Russia on the east; Hungary and Austria on the south and Germany on the west. The important cities are Prague, Bratislava, Brno, and Plezen. Czechoslovakia has a reputation for its intensive farming, its Skoda iron works, Bohemian glassware and its richly decorated pottery. It is self-sufficient as far as food is concerned for it produces, wheat, rye, oats, corn, barley and hops; grows such fruits as apples, pears, peaches, plums, cherries and apricots; raises cattle, sheep, poultry and pigs.

Canada considered Czechoslovakia one as of her favourite countries in Eastern Europe; the other one being Poland. Like Poland and Yugoslavia it was carved out of the three former empires: Hapsburg, German and Russian. Under the leadership of Thomas Masaryk and Eduard Benes it experienced a rather stable government, but unlike Poland, it enjoyed reasonable prosperity. Like Poland it was a victim of Hitler's aggressive foreign policy in 1938-39 but it did not suffer the untold atrocities that the Poles did.

Czechoslovakia was the only East European country that had a "free and unfettered election." For two years, (1946-1948) Czechoslovakia enjoyed most of the amenities and freedoms found in the West: Western newspapers were conspicuous in the newspaper racks, people listened to Radio Free Europe, and enjoyed freedom of assembly and expression.[15] In February 1948 all this changed when the communists engineered a *coup* under the leadership of Klement Gottwald and installed a communist regime.(Map.)

"E"

The fifth largest East European country, Hungary, had in 1990 a population of 10,365,000 and an area of 93,030 km^2. It is bounded on the north by Czechoslovakia; on the east by Russia and Romania; on the south by Yugoslavia and on the west by Austria. The chief cities are Budapest, Miskolc, Debrecen and Pecs. Her main industries are agriculture, iron and steel production, fertilizers, chemicals, paper and textiles. Like Czechoslovakia it is self-sufficient in food as it grows wheat, barley, rye oats and sugar beets. The Hungarian farmers also raise cattle, horses, hogs, and sheep. Since the end of the Second World War it has become more industrialized producing coal, oil and iron ore.

Although strictly speaking Hungarians (Magyars) do not belong to the Slavic group of nations, they are frequently lumped with them. In 1849 Hungary was recognized as an equal partner in the Dual Monarchy whereby the Emperor of Austria was also the king of Hungary. Following the defeat of Germany and Austria in World War I, the two countries became independent.

The interwar period was a difficult time for these two powers as they encountered instability, ethnic tensions and economic turmoil. The unsettled conditions made it possible for Bela Kun, a communist leader, to make some headway but soon found little support for his communist regime. After the Second World War the communists with the help of the Red Army and the Soviet secret police had entrenched themselves in Hungary by 1947.

"F"

Bulgaria is the last and the smallest of the six East European countries having a population of 8,900,000 people living in an area of 110,910 km^2. Bulgaria is bounded on the north by the Danube River and Romania; on the east by Black Sea; on the south by Greece and Turkey and on the west by Yugoslavia. See the map) Its main cities are Sofia, the capital, Plovdid and Varna. It is primarily agricultural country producing abundant grain, vegetable and fruit crops most of them in the fertile valleys of the Danube and Maritsa Rivers. Many farmers specialize in raising domestic animals chiefly horses, cattle, hogs, sheep and poultry. It also has included such industries as manufacturing of chemicals, the textile industry, iron production and sugar refineries.

Like Poland, Bulgaria has a rather long history, being absorbed by the Byzantine Empire and then conquered by the Turks in the 14th century and remaining under this jurisdiction for over 500 years. Her close ally Russia freed her when she became independent as the result of Russia's victory over Turkey in 1877-78.[16] She was closely linked with Russia because of her history, Orthodox religion and language. When the communists gained control of the country they imposed on it a Soviet version of government, economics and culture. Her foreign policy also closely followed that of the Soviet Union. (See map.)

Divergence in Eastern Europe

Many North Americans considered Eastern Europe a monolithic entity slavishly and hopelessly following Moscow's political, economic, social and foreign policy models. During Stalin's time there was considerable uniformity, but beginning with Yugoslavia in 1949, satellite countries who chafed under their repressive regimes found ingenious ways of becoming less dependent on the Kremlin. After the death of Stalin in 1953 and particularly after Khrushchev's denunciation of the dictator in 1956 satellite countries discreetly found ways of proclaiming themselves communist in public while at the same time adopting free market ideas and striking out on their own in their foreign policies. In economic innovations Hungary and Yugoslavia led the rest of the Soviet-bloc countries. A brain-child of Janos Kadar The New Economic Mechanism[17] was introduced into Hungary in 1968. It was a departure of the command economy as it emphasized decentralization of authority, and the use of incentives to increase productivity and the quality of goods. The Yugoslav Workers' Self-Management model also stressed decentralization and placed the onus of success on the workers who were encouraged, through social ownership, social planning, and the business cooperation of peasants, to create an atmosphere of personal satisfaction..

Romania became a deviant from the communist model by adopting an independent foreign policy.[18] Under Nicolae Ceausescu, she did not always follow other satellites in voting with them at the United Nations. She did not participate in the invasion of Czechoslovakia in 1968. In domestic affairs, however, she religiously adhered to the basic tenets of communism.

Poland was the most rebellious member of the communist family. Fortified by the strong support of the Roman Catholics in Poland and by Pope John Paul II, most of the Poles formed an unofficial opposition to the ruling Polish United Workers' Party. Unlike the Czechoslovaks, Poles expressed their grievances openly on political, religious and economic matters. The unprecedented growth of the Solidarity Movement in 1980 indicated the unity and the determination of the people to achieve political and economic freedoms. Despite the many restraints, Poland enjoyed more freedom than any of the other five communist states.

Notes

[1] R.H. Osborne, *East-Central Europe,* Chatto & Windus, London, 1967, See Chapter 2 and Hugh Seton-Watson, Eastern *Europe Between the Wars, 1918-1941,* Harper & Row Publishers, 1962, pp. xv-xii of the Introduction.

[2] Vernon V. Aspaturian, "Eastern Europe in World Perspective" in *Communism in Eastern Europe,* edited by Teresa Rakowska-Harmstone and Andrew Gyorgy, Indiana University Press, 1979, p. 1.

[3] Aloysius Balawyder, *In the Clutches of the Kremlin, Canadian-East-European Relations 1945-1962*, published and distributed by Columbia University Press, 2000, see Chapter VIII.

[4] H. Gordon Skilling, "Canada and Eastern Europe," *Canadian Slavonic Papers,* vol viii, 1966, pp. 3-16.

[5] *Ibid.*

[7] *Ibid.* Peyton Lyon's discussion on Skilling's paper, pp. 20-21.

[8] *Ibid.* Derry Novak's discussion on Skilling's paper, pp. 40-41.

[9] *Ibid.* Adam Bromke's discussion on Skilling's paper. pp. 43-44.

[10] At the Belgrade Conference held in October 1977 Klaus Goldschlag, Canadian chief delegate stressed the issue of family reunification.

[11] See *Statistics Abstract of the World,* edited by Marlita A Reddy, Gale Research Inc. For size and population see page 166 (Canada) and pages 166, 828, 247 806, 109, 834, 132, 752, 229, for East European Countries. Statistics on boundaries, industries and occupations are based on volumes 2, 3, 7, 1, and 14 of the *American Educator Encyclopedia,* under the headings of the six East Euro-pean countries.

[12] M. Dziewanowski, *POLAND in the 20th Century,* Columbia University Press, 1977, Chapter I "Roots of the Present" p. 1.

[13] R.H. Osborne, *op. cit.* p. 289.

[14] Robin Allison Remington, "Yugoslavia" found in *Communism in Eastern Europe,* edited by Teresa Rakowska-Harmstone et al, p. 214.

[15] Aloysius Balawyder, *In the Clutches of the Kremlin, op.cit.* p. 38.

[16] Robert R. King, "Bulgaria" *Communism in Eastern Europe,* p. 169.

[17] Bennett Kovrig, "Hungary" *ibid.* pp. 88-90.

[18] Robert R. King, "Romania" *ibid.* pp. 161-166.

II. GETTING TO KNOW ONE ANOTHER

The Iron Curtain prevented a free exchange of people and ideas between East and West and created an atmosphere of suspicion and distrust. There was a general feeling that the communist regimes were evil and contacts with them ought to be avoided. Western newspapers and magazines were forbidden in the communist-controlled countries. During the post-Stalin years, (1945-1953) there was little immigration, a deliberate policy of the communist governments of the Soviet Union and her satellites to minimize contacts with the capitalist and imperialist West. Even diplomats from the West had difficulty meeting communist government officials. A Canadian diplomat noted that he had only three contacts with Polish government officials during his two years in Warsaw from 1951 to 1953.[1] Ordinarily foreign diplomats would have regular personal with their counterparts.

Though some of the rigid regulations were modified after the death of Stalin, the general atmosphere did not improve significantly. Diplomats and their family members were continuously harassed: to travel beyond twenty-five miles required authorization from the regime and even when authorization was obtained from the communist authorities secret police continued to tail the diplomats. The communist regimes attempted to jam broadcasts from Radio Free Europe, the Voice of America, the BBC and the CBC International Service.

The West including Canada was ever vigilant in issuing visas to members of the communist party. Ottawa carefully screened new European diplomats earmarked for Canada, for she was concerned about the security risks the East European diplomats posed for Canada and the danger they might present to the Canadian East European communities. The RCMP kept tabs on the personnel working in East European legations as well as on the members of the Communist Party of Canada. Generally they contacted Canadians who were planning to travel to the Soviet Union or to Eastern Europe, informing him/her of some of the pitfalls a Canadian might encounter. At the same time they attempted to find more information on individuals who were interested in the Soviet Union and in her satellites.[2]

The ingrained prejudices against the communists had certain legitimate bases in fact. During the inter-war period members of the Communist Party of Canada encouraged strikes and lockouts.[3] Canadians labeled the communists as atheists and anarchists. The alarming pronouncements from the Comintern and at times from the Communist Party of Canada confirmed the commonly-held opinion that sooner or later the communists would try to replace the Canadian democratic government. It is no wonder that the RCMP interrogated travelers who planned to travel to Eastern Europe or who just returned from this area.

Influence of Canadian Diplomats

Notwithstanding the differences between the East and the West, Canadian diplomats exercised considerable influence in the countries they served. By their professional and friendly contacts with the personnel in East European posts they were able to cultivate friendly relations with Eastern-bloc countries. Although the Canadian diplomatic corps was not large compared with that of Great Britain or the United States the quality of the officers was second to none. One of the officers, Jack McCordick, served in Canadian legations in Moscow, Prague, Warsaw and Belgrade and opened posts in Budapest and Bucharest. He was in a position to inform the Canadian government of some of the differences between the peoples of the communist bloc countries. According to him, the Czechoslovaks learned to be cautious, whereas the Poles "got on the horse and charged." He considered the Poles very distinctive; "they were very Polish in every thing they said and did." And they did things with great determination. (See the Appendices.)

Another great admirer of the Polish people and culture was Hamilton Southam, the first Canadian ambassador to Poland. He agreed with McCordick in pointing out that Canada's relations with Poland were "special" for three reasons; namely, that there were more ethnic Poles in Canada than ethnic Czechoslovaks, Yugoslavs or Hungarians. Canadians and Poles fought side by side in the Second World War and shared similar values.[4] Another diplomat, A.F. Hart, who spent two years in Poland in the 1950s and was Canada's ambassador to Poland in 1975, voiced the same opinion.

Many of the contacts and negotiations between Canadian and East European diplomats were informal. The policy adopted in the solution of the detention of the Polish Art Treasures was first discussed and agreed upon by the Polish diplomat to the United Nations, Manfred Lachs and the Canadian representative at the United Nations, John Holmes. Yugoslav and Hungarian diplomats met regularly with Canadian diplomats in the lobbies of the United Nations particularly during the late 1970s and 1980s, the flowering years of the détente. The United Nations buzzed with discussions among the delegates. The free exchange of ideas helped to impress upon the Soviet and East European representatives that human beings, regardless of their ideologies, are basically the same and that every person longs for a "good" life, a life that will bring him/her happiness and peace.

During the time of détente there was a slight movement of people from Eastern Europe. Tourism received a great boost. There was a gradual loosening of restrictions on the movements of people in all East European countries but especially between Poland and Hungary on the one hand and Canada, on the other.

Cultural, Scientific and Academic Exchanges

Beginning in the 1960s, the West had shown interest in exchanges with the Soviet Union and her satellites. The first Western country that signed a formal agreement with the Soviet Union in 1966 was France followed by similar agreements with Great Britain, Austria, Belgium, Denmark, Sweden and Finland. Canada concluded two agreements with the Soviet Union in 1971, one on industrial applications and the other on General Exchanges.[5]

These exchanges and agreements with the Soviet Union and the West were vital for a better mutual understanding and co-operation. Regardless of the nature or the size of these exchanges, each side had an opportunity to appreciate the needs and the aspirations of other governments and people. For the most part each side began to realize how similar they were. Friendly relations with the Soviet Union spilled over to the countries of Eastern Europe. Canada began to sign bilateral and multilateral academic, scientific and cultural agreements with communist bloc countries. Furthermore, by signing the Helsinki Accords in 1975 Canada agreed to the provisions contained in Basket III that obligated her to improve the opportunities for the exchange of scientific and technical information.

Before the governments became involved in these exchanges, universities were the organizers and promoters of them. By 1976 Canada entered into official exchanges with Hungary, Poland and Yugoslavia in reciprocal scholarship programs.[6] The National Research Council and the Social Sciences and Humanities Research Council provided the funding for such research in Canada and abroad. Competition was open to both Canadian and European scholars.

As in the case of Canadian-Soviet exchanges, East Europeans generally opted for physical sciences, economics and mathematics, whereas Canadians preferred social sciences. East Europeans took advantage of these exchanges because they had a command of either French or English as well as their own native language. Only a small number of Canadians had a reading and/or a spoken knowledge of one or more East European languages.

There were other differences. Canadian students found it difficult to get accommodation in Eastern Europe and most of the institutions in the Soviet bloc countries provided meager scholarships for foreign students. Students of Polish origin were given an opportunity to learn about their Polish heritage by attending six-week summer seminars at either the Jagillonian University in Cracow or the Catholic University at Lublin under the auspices of the Reymont Foundation.[7] At these Polish institutions students studied history, culture and economics. Despite some of the shortcomings, students did gain an appreciation of the culture and the traditions of Poland.

Cultural exchanges provided other important means to appreciate one another's culture and traditions. In December 1977 the McGill University Chamber Orchestra made in December 1977 a concert tour of Poland, Czechoslovakia and Budapest.[8] The well-known Stratford Festival Theatre performed before large audiences in Czechoslovakia and Poland. In return the Poznan boys' choir and the Warsaw Philharmonic orchestra received a warm welcome in Canada for their concert rendition. Again in 1978 the Czechoslovak group called the "Black Theatre" toured Ontario and Quebec.

By far it was Expo 67, Canada's centennial celebration of her origin as a nation that made Canada a showcase.[9] Three Soviet bloc countries, Czechoslovakia, Yugoslavia and the Soviet Union had pavilions at Expo. Thousands and thousands of Canadians and citizens of many countries flocked to Montreal to participate in the gala affair. Presidents, prime ministers, artists and performers took part in the celebration. All heads of states, except President Charles de Gaulle, were ushered to Ottawa, where they received an official welcome. Among other distinguished visitors[10] were Queen Juliana of Holland, Austrian President Franz Jonas, Deputy Minister of Soviet Foreign Affairs of the USSR. V.V. Kuznetzov, Belgian Prince Albert and General Secretary of the Communist Party of Czechoslovakia, Antonin Novotny. The air buzzed with jubilation, harmony and joy as visitors from all over the world met, exchanged greetings and smiles. The hospitable atmosphere gave the impression that the Cold War was a thing of the past.

Of all the pavilions at the Expo, the Czechoslovak one was universally singled out as the most beautiful and interesting. There were long queues of people waiting to get in. The wonderment of what they saw and experienced was evident in their faces. The structure of and the performances in the Czech pavilion invited everyone to reflect how knowledge and the skills, if combined, could enlarge mankind's horizon. They were challenged to live in harmony and peace. Sadly, a year after Expo this harmony was shattered by the Soviet-led invasion of this beautiful country.

Round Table Discussions

One of the most successful means of exchanging views and aspirations was organized by the Canadian Institute of International Affairs (CIIA) and the Polish Institute of International Affairs (PIIA). Two of the conferences were held in Canada in 1967 and 1972 and two in Poland in 1969 and 1974. At these conferences a variety of topics were discussed, the most important being: East-West trade, disarmament, NATO, Warsaw Pact Alliance, European security and cultural exchanges.[11]

The fourth Round Table discussion chaired by the Polish representative, Marion Dobrosielski, focused on the Helsinki Accords and their role in European security.[12] The Polish delegation supported a movement that called for the abolition of the existing alliances. The Canadian delegate chairman listened with interest to the suggestions given by the Polish spokesman, but felt that the immediate concern for Canadians was family reunification and a free movement of peoples in all countries of Eastern Europe.

With the signing of the Helsinki Accords, Round Table discussions became redundant because there were now ample opportunities in the three baskets for meaningful contacts. However, the Accords did not prevent Canadian universities from signing academic and cultural agreements. For instance, Carleton University and the Hungarian Institute of Cultural Relations signed an agreement of exchanges in 1974. Two years later, Canada entered into an official reciprocal program agreement not only with Hungary but also with Yugoslavia.

Parliamentary Visits

Another effective means of developing trust and confidence was the exchange of parliamentary delegations. Policy makers and shakers had an opportunity to observe on the spot, how different parliaments operated. Many misconceptions were corrected and new information gleaned about the other side. Upon returning home to their respective countries these delegates shared their observations with other members of parliament.

In 1975 a seventeen-member delegation led by James Jerome, the speaker of the Canadian House of Commons, along with Senator Raymond Perrault made an official eight-day visit to the Soviet Union. Earlier that year a Canadian parliamentary delegation was a guest of the Polish parliament (Sejm). It was Canada's turn to welcome East European parliamentary delegations. In 1976 Canada was the host to delegations from Yugoslavia, Hungary and the Soviet Union. Three years later Canadian parliamentarians traveled to Prague to attend the International Parliamentary Union's meeting.[13]

On account of unsettling events involving the Soviet Union and/or East European countries, exchanges and visits were put on hold or curtailed. During the Soviet-led invasion of Czechoslovakia, 1968, the Soviet invasion of Afghanistan, 1979, and the imposition of martial law in Poland, 1981, cultural, scientific and academic exchanges were left in abeyance. The leaders realized the benefits of such exchanges and hastened to restore these exchanges.

Bilateral Visits and Meetings

The Helsinki Accords opened the doors to countless bilateral visits and meetings of businessmen, economists, technicians, and experts in mining, lumbering, fishing and agriculture. Beginning in the mid-seventies Canada was inundated with East European experts, and high-ranking civil servants who were seeking information on areas vital to their country's prosperity. Such meetings sustained and increased the existing détente. (Further details on bilateral relations are found in Chapter VI.)

Notes

[1] A.F. Hart interviewed by the author May 6, 1984 said that there was very little contact between the Warsaw government and the Canadian legation.

[2] It was also a means used by RCMP to keep track of the individuals who traveled to communist countries.

[3] Aloysius Balawyder's *Canadian-Soviet Relations Between the World Wars,* University of Toronto Press, 1972, Chapter 10.

[4] Author's interview with Jack McCordick, December 8, 1984. He also served as Canadian ambassador to Poland.

[5] For details on scientific and technological exchanges between Canada and the Soviet Union see Jocelyn M Ghent's article in Aloysius Balawyder's edited book, *Canadian-Soviet Relations, 1939-1980,* Mosaic Press, Toronto, and Chapter VIII.

[6] *Canadian Annual Review,* 1976.

[7] "Academic Exchanges and Cultural Co-operation" From the Canadian Embassy in Warsaw, January 21, 1971, RG 25 volume 10839 file 20-1-2 Poland, Vol. 7, DEA, NAC.

[8] See Canadian-Polish Relations Chronology, *ibid.*

[9] Canadian Embassy in Prague to USSEA, April 5, 1967, RG 25, volume 10502, file 55-73-Mtl-2 Czech NAC.

[10] *Ibid.*

[11] Aloysius Balawyder, *The Maple Leaf and the White Eagle,* pp. 180-181.

[12] CSCE, "Canadian Round Table" December 21, 1972, RG 25 volume 10839, file 20-1-2 POL, NAC.

[13] *Canadian Annual Report,* 1979, Ottawa, NAC.

III. CANADA'S REACTION TO CRISES

Canada's reaction to crises in Eastern Europe must be taken in the context of East-West relations. Events in the West or in the communist-controlled countries had an important bearing on Canada's relations with the Soviet Union and her satellites.[1] As a member of NATO and the United Nations Canada reacted to the crises in Eastern Europe and generally followd in the footsteps of these two organizations but at the same time adhered to her national interests.

With the exceptions of Yugoslavia after 1948 and Romania under Nicholae Ceausecu the foreign policies of the Eastern bloc countries followed closely the foreign policy of the Soviet Union, the leading power in the Warsaw Treaty Organization. In the United Nations and in its agencies, the satellites supported the Soviet Union. In an attempt to camouflage the control of Moscow over her satellites, the Soviet Union urged East European countries to speak in the United Nations on her behalf. The constitutions of Eastern Europe were more or less copies of the constitution of the Soviet Union and the economies of Eastern Europe were linked to the economy of the Soviet Union through COMECON.

The Czech Coup

Up to 1948 the communist grip over Czechoslovakia was not as tight as the grip exercised by the communists over Poland, Hungary, Bulgaria, and Romania. Although the key government positions including that of a premier were in the hands of the communists there was considerable amount of freedom.[2] Western newspapers were available in Prague and in other cities. People listened to foreign radio broadcasts and travel in the country was not restricted. Czechoslovakia was a bridge between the East and the West.

Unfortunately this bridge did not last very long. Gottwald and his Party realized that the communists would not do well in the forthcoming elections decided to act decisively to create a crisis. His minister of the interior dismissed high-ranking police officers. To express their protest to this move twelve members of the Czechoslovak government resigned. Gottwald used this occasion to ask President Benes to replace the ministers with his communist members. Benes reluctantly agreed to this. By so doing he closed the last window to the West as the communists took control of the struggling democracy.

The Czech *coup* ignited strong reactions in the West. The allies condemned the action of the communists and sympathized with the Czechoslovaks. The Canadian delegate at the United Nations, A.G.L. McNaughton, supported a Chilean motion, which called for an investigation of the role of the Soviet Union in the *coup.* In the House of Commons, the Canadian secretary for External Affairs, Louis St. Laurent, condemned the despicable act calling it "a frightening case history of communist totalitarianism in action." [3]

The immediate effect of the *coup* was the formation of the North Atlantic Treaty Organization (NATO). The purpose of the alliance was to discourage future communist aggression and to protect all sovereign states. Canada was a strong supporter of NATO and one of her diplomats, Escott Reid, helped in the formulation of its policy. Generally, the Canadian government sought guidance from NATO when trying to discern the best way to deal with the members of the Soviet bloc.

Poland and Forces for Change

In June 1956 steel plant workers in Poznan went on strike demanding better working conditions and higher wages. But it was more than a strike; deep down in the Polish memories the entire issue of legitimacy of the communist regime and independence were re-activated. Poles wanted the freedom to decide what was best for themselves rather than have decisions imposed on them. Polish police crushed the strike, killing sixty-four people and wounding several hundreds. .

From this tragedy some positive events emerged. Poland got a new leader. The Polish United Workers' Party (PUWP) choose Wladyslaw Gomulka as their new secretary general of their Party much against the wishes of Moscow. Nikita Khrushchev and the Soviet politburo reluctantly agreed to the choice of the leader. This was an outstanding victory for the embattled Poles who suffered enormously at the hands of the Soviet masters. For two years (1956-1958) Gomulka was acclaimed a hero as he granted the people some political, economic and religious freedom. His concessions were temporary, however, for under Moscow's pressure he began to follow a more conservative path to socialism. By 1970 he lost the "hero" image and was now considered by the Poles a stooge of Moscow.

Hungarian Bloody Revolution

The Polish people's spirit of independence influenced the Hungarians' revolt in 1956. Students in Budapest in particular followed keenly the events in Poland. Among the 225 demands the Hungarian revolutionaries wanted, the most important ones were national independence, the withdrawal of Soviet troops from Hungary, economic reforms and free elections.[4] The leader for these reforms was premier Imre Nagy. The Soviet Union was afraid of these reforms and sent her tanks to crush the revolution. An estimated 200,000 Hungarians crossed the borders and left Hungary; 37,566 came to Canada. As in the case of 1304 Czechoslovak refugees who were admitted into Canada in 1948, the Canadian government waved some security, health and job requirements for the Hungarians.

Canada, alarmed at the treatment of the freedom-loving people joined other countries by protesting against the Soviet action in Hungary. L.B. Pearson, the then Canadian secretary of state for External Affairs, participated in the United Nations debate where nation after nation condemned the Soviet Union for betraying Hungarian students and workers by repressing their freedoms. The Canadian Prime Minister, Louis Saint-Laurent, expressed Canada's horror at the brutality of the Soviet army and secret police. In a letter to the Soviet premier, N.A. Bulganin, St Laurent asked the premier to do all he could to alleviate the sufferings of the Hungarian people. The Soviet premier dismissed the charges by claiming them to be "one-sided, tendentious and subjective." He maintained that reactionary forces with outside help tried to overthrow the Hungarian "democratic regime." [5]

Soviet-Led Invasion of Czechoslovakia

Twenty years after the Czech *coup* and a dozen years after the Hungarian Revolt, the Soviet Union was again involved in repressing a democratic political movement, which endorsed democracy, independence and freedom. There were similarities and differences between the 1948 and the 1968 events. In both cases the Soviet Union perpetrated or supported the crisis. The communist party of Czechoslovakia prepared the grounds for the 1948 *coup* and carried it out to its completion, whereas in 1968 the Soviet Union with the help of her satellites, Poland, Bulgaria, East Germany and Hungary, interfered in the internal affairs of the Czechoslovakia. In both instances fear seemed to dictate the move. In 1948 the communist party of Czechoslovakia feared that in the pending elections communists would lose very badly and so they pre-empted a *coup.* In 1968 the Soviet Union and her four satellites feared that the democratic movement under the leadership of Alexander Dubcek might encourage people in their countries to demand more freedom and even independence.[6]

In 1948 the *coup* was aimed at overthrowing the existing democratically elected coalition. But in 1968 the liberal wing of the Czechoslovak Communist Party initiated steps towards more political, social and economic freedom. One of the great hurdles to the reforms was Antonin Novotny, a former general secretary of the Communist Party. He was ousted from the leadership of the Party in January 1968 and replaced by Alexander Dubcek.

The change in leadership ushered in a period of democratization. Open debates on television and radio were held; press censorship was abolished and former victims of repression detailed the torture to which they were subjected and the so-called enemies of the state were rehabilitated. A well-known novelist, Ludvik Vaculik drew up a statement known as "2000 Words" signed by seventy workers and intellectuals calling for the abolition of the "leading role" of the communist party and the introduction of a multi-party system of government. This statement was published in the Prague journal "*Literani Listy* on June 27, 1968.[7] Moscow denounced the article labeling it "counter revolutionary."

The Soviet general secretary of the Party, Leonid Brezhnev, attempted to dampen the growing movement towards more freedom and independence. An important meeting was held between Czechoslovak and the Soviet Politburo members on July 29, 1968 at Cierna nad Tisou at which time Dubcek defended his proposed reforms. Brezhnev countered Dubcek's arguments at the meeting of the leaders of all the Soviet bloc countries, who met in Bratislava to hear the Soviet version of events that had taken place between the Party leaders of Czechoslovakia and the Soviet Union. He described the impasse as neither side wanted to back down from its positions. Moscow waved its heavy hand and pressured Dubcek to correct his errors and return to the "socialist" norms or face drastic results. Rather suddenly in the night of August 20 to August 21,600, 000 troops of the Soviet Union, Poland, East Germany, Hungary and Bulgaria crossed into Czechoslovakia without much resistance. Dubcek and the president of the republic were summoned to Moscow and given directives. Dubcek continued as the secretary general of the Communist Party until March 1969 at which time Gustav Husak replaced him.

Reaction to the Invasion

The Czechoslovak minister of Foreign Affairs denounced the invasion and vehemently denied the allegation that the Czechoslovak government had invited the Warsaw Pact armies. Many communist parties, particularly the French and the Italian ones, condemned the invasion. And so did the Communist Party of Canada. Moscow used a policy, called the Brezhnev Doctrine, which all allegedly provided the Soviet Union a trumped rationale to invade Czechoslovakia under the pretext of preventing her from breaking away from the "socialist" family and becoming independent.

Canada reacted quickly. On the same day that the invasion began, Mitchell Sharp, the minister for External Affairs, in the absence of prime minister Pierre Trudeau, expressed on behalf of his government disappointment at Moscow's action, for in his opinion, he maintained that this would "be a great set-back to the growth of détente." [8] A few days later, Trudeau sent a message to Brezhnev via the Soviet's ambassador to Canada:

> The invasion and occupation of Czechoslovakia constitute a flagrant breach of the principle of non-intervention to which the Soviet Union itself professes to subscribe. It is also (a) tragedy for all the people who prize human freedom and national independence, and I am confident that its significance will not be lost on the peoples of Eastern Europe and even (on) the Soviet Union...As far as the Atlantic Alliance is concerned...the Soviet occupation of Czechoslovakia constitutes a serious setback to our dialogue.[9]

The issue of the invasion of Czechoslovakia was introduced into the United Nations and in the Canadian House of Commons. The Canadian representative, George Ignatiev, supported a resolution in the United Nations General Assembly condemning the Soviet Union for her interference in the internal affairs of Czechoslovakia.[10] Although the resolution was vetoed by the Soviet Union the Canadian representative did not hesitate to introduce a second resolution calling on the international body to guarantee safety to Alexander Dubcek.[11] This was passed.

Canada was shaken by the events leading to and following the Soviet-led invasion. It appeared to Canada that freedom would never come to Eastern Europe unless and until the Soviet Union agreed to permit her satellites to be free and independent. In the meantime Canada attempted to demonstrate what true democracy was. She allowed ten thousand Czechoslovak refugees to immigrate to Canada without the usual rigorous health and security scrutiny.[12] In addition, the Canadian government made two million dollars available for the resettlement of the refugees.

In union with NATO countries Canada agreed to impose sanctions on the Soviet Union.[13] New cultural, scientific and academic exchanges were suspended. However, existing exchanges were allowed to continue. A meeting between the Soviet and Canadian Institutes of Forestry was cancelled. There was a general feeling that sanctions did more harm to the cultural and scientific community than any benefits that could result from the imposition of sanctions on the Soviet Union.

By 1970 the relations between the Soviet Union and the West became more or less normal. However, the negotiations on the treaty banning nuclear weapons were delayed. Détente was the main victim as the ugly head of suspicion and distrust came to the surface again. A mild cold war engendered an atmosphere encouraging an arms race between the two super-powers. Both sides were convinced that confidence building must replace armament building but hesitated to take the first move.

Genesis of Polish Resistance

Polish history is characterized by determined efforts for national survival.[14] Beginning with the origin of the Polish state in 966 the Polish people struggled against the Swedes, Ottoman Turks and Moscovy to remain free and independent. The marriage in 1386 of the Lithuanian Duke Jagiello to Queen Jadwiga enlarged and strengthened the newly-formed Polish-Lithuanian Commonwealth. In 1410 the Teutonic Knights at the battle of Grunwald challenged the Commonwealth. The resounding victory of the Polish Commonwealth armies over the greatest military power at that time, the Order of the Teutonic Knights, put an end to the ambitions of this organization. Two hundred years later the Turks challenged the Commonwealth. In l683 Jan Sobieski won a brilliant victory against the Moslem Turks and salvaged Christian Europe.

This victory did not eliminate other challenges. Prussia, Russia and Austria took advantage of a weakened the Commonwealth and its internal intrigues and partitioned Poland in 1772, 1793 and 1795. The three partitioning powers ruled Poland for 123 years except for eight years (1807-1815) when Napoleon Bonaparte created a semi-independent state, the Duchy of Warsaw. During these years of occupation, the Polish culture, language and traditions were preserved. The Treaty of Versailles (1919) re-created Poland only to be occupied by Nazi Germany and the Soviet Union during the Second World War (1939-1935). Despite the tyrannical and despotic Nazi and Communist masters, the Poles refused to surrender their spirit of freedom to the enemies.

Unfortunately at the Yalta Conference in 1945, Poland as well as the other five East European countries was placed under the jurisdiction of the Soviet Union. In other words another occupation took place, this time under the auspices of the Communist Party of the USSR. The Soviet imposed settlement was not accepted by the Soviet-bloc countries. The Poles considered the regime illegitimate because it failed to "penetrate" deeply into the hearts of the people.[15] Even in the minds of the members of the Polish United Workers' Party there remained a dichotomy of loyalty to their country, on one hand, and loyalty to the Soviet Union on the other. For many Poles membership to the Party was just a certificate for gainful employment and not an acceptance of the terms of the Yalta Conference.

Challenges to the Regime

Prior to 1956 Poles exercised passive resistance to the imposed regime, but during the détente the resistance grew from a mild degree of non-acceptance of the communist regimes to an open defiance. In Poland this resistance was evident in the insistence on the termination of collectivization of land, better Church-State relations, more freedom of the press and significant economic reforms. At the beginning of Gomulka's regime there were symbolic and some real evidences of religious, political, social and economic freedoms only to evaporate during the latter years of his term of office.

But the Poles refused to go back; they took the advantage of the détente atmosphere and particularly the Helsinki Accords and boldly pressed forward. The workers demanded better working conditions and higher wages. Instead of heeding these demands the regime increased the price of food and consumer goods by thirty percent. In December 1970 massive and bloody demonstrations took place in the Baltic coastal cities of Gdansk, Gdynia, Sopot and Sczczecin. Gomulka's regime reacted by using force to quell the riots. Forty-five people were killed and 1,165 wounded.[16] The government withdrew the price increase; Gomulka resigned and was replaced as the secretary general of the PUWP by Edward Gierek, the former boss of the Communist party in Silesia.

Upon taking office Gierek projected an image of a reformer and an enthusiastic manager.[17] To increase productivity he modernized certain industries and to satisfy the public clamor for consumer goods he imported rather liberally goods from abroad. He decentralized the management of enterprises providing a semblance of market economy. National income rose by ten percent. To placate the farmers he abolished compulsory delivery of agricultural products, established the indivisibility of small farms and did away with fixed prices on farm products.

These real and cosmetic reforms did not fully meet the needs of the people. The nagging scepter of imposed domination by the Soviet Union prevented the Poles from accepting Gierek's attempts to keep workers, students, intellectuals and the Church satisfied. Throughout Poland opposition multiplied each group having its own reasons for dissatisfaction. In 1976 the PUWP joined the intellectuals in opposing the ideological offensive aimed at drawing up a new constitution based on the Soviet model.[18] Cardinal Wyszynski and the Catholic Episcopate threw their weight behind the opposition. Because of the insistent pressure the regime modified its constitutional amendments. But the simmering revolt broke out in another quarter. The workers joined by students and intellectuals objected strenuously to the ill treatment of workers at the Ursus and Radom plants and formed on September 27, 1976 a Committee for Defense of the Workers (KOR). A year later KOR was expanded to a Committee for Social Defense (KSS-KOR).

The KOR organization was a social body and not a political one thus preserving an image of detachment. It did not have any formal structure and it conducted its activities openly. It freely offered encouragement, legal advice and financial assistance to those who had under gone political persecution or prosecution. Its influence lay in its numerous declarations, communiqués and appeals. Another organization that came into being in 1977 was the Movement for the Defense of Human and Civil Rights (ROPCIO) a non-Marxist group, whose purpose was to be a mouthpiece for the innocent citizens who were detained, mistreated or persecuted.

These organizations and opposition groups were the precursors of the Solidarity movement. In 1980 Solidarity made public its twenty-one demands; many of which dealt with "bread and butter issues," but some touched upon the very core of democratic rights.[19] Keeping in mind that Poland was a communist country whose government never had permitted independent unions to exist much less to have the right to strike. Such a move was vigorously opposed. The workers were demanding not only to unionize but were also asking for greater freedoms of the press, speech and assembly. The new government under Stanislaw Kania, caved in and signed an agree-ment with Solidarity on August 31, 1980. The Agreement did not solve the nagging problem. The workers demanded further reforms and freedoms. The government refused to budge.

The world was waiting to see who would move next, Solidarity or the Communist government. In the meantime Soviet and satellite troops resumed their maneuvers near the Polish borders giving the indication that either Russian forces might invade Poland or that martial law could be imposed. General Wojcech Jaruszelski replaced Kania in February 1980 as the secretary general of PWUP. To political observers it was apparent that the Polish government was about to declare martial law rather than permit the Soviet forces to invade Poland. On December 13, 1981during the night all telephones were cut, thousands of Solidarity leaders and their supporters were arrested or detained and tanks and military vehicles crowded the streets of Warsaw and large cities.

Canada's Reaction to the Martial Law

Canadians of Polish origin reacted immediately and vigorously. Canadian-Polish Congress, an umbrella organization for the Polish community condemned the imposition of the martial law labeling it as an infringement of human rights. It urged Ottawa to send a clear message to the Warsaw regime stating that such intervention was not acceptable. The secretary of state for Foreign Affairs, Mark McGuigan, agreed with the statement of the Canadian-Polish Congress knowing full well that in his constituency there were many Canadian ethnic Poles and other Slavic groups who opposed martial law.[20]

Prime Minister Pierre Trudeau added confusion to this event when he was interviewed by Bruce Phillips. The Prime Minister seemed to deplore what was happening in Poland not because democratic rights of the Polish people were trampled but because relations with the Soviet Union would probably suffer a setback and the existing détente would be effected. He went further by labeling the Solidarity just another labour union, which, from his Canadian experience of unions, continually demanded unrealistic wages and benefits. Trudeau went as far as intimating that the imposition of the martial might have prevented the Soviet invasion of Poland.[21]

Trudeau's attitude put the minister for External Affairs, in an awkward position. MacGuigan was reluctant to criticize his boss and yet he did not want to alienate his constituents. He assured the House of Commons that his government was working in concert with NATO partners to bring about a suitable solution to the Polish crisis.

Four motions were introduced in the House of Commons under standing order 43 condemning the Polish government's violation of the Helsinki Agreement. Three of these motions introduced by Conservative members of parliament and one by a Liberal which received unanimous approval.[22] One of the motions urged the Polish government to end martial law, grant amnesty to the imprisoned and to begin meaningful negotiations with the Solidarity and the Roman Catholic Church.

Outside the House of Commons McGuigan vigorously chastised the Warsaw government for imposing the martial law. Speaking at the Conference of Security and Co-operation in Europe he emphasized that the Polish government violated Principle VII of the Helsinki Agreement signed by Poland and thirty-three other countries when they agreed to "respect human rights and fundamental freedoms including the freedom of thought, conscience, religion or belief without distinction as to race, sex, language or religion."[23] He accused the Polish government of detaining thousands of Polish citizens without a due process of law. Some of the detainees were forbidden to contact their families and friends and some were forced under threats of losing their jobs to sign statements of renouncing membership to the Solidarity organization. McGuigan encouraged all nations to permit the Polish people resolve their problems themselves, for they were the only ones who could do so effectively.

NATO countries including Canada imposed sanctions on the Polish government. Scheduled exchanges and meetings were suspended; loans for Poland were cancelled, trade negotiations were placed on the shelf. In 1983 Polish government lifted the martial law but maintained some of the restrictive martial law measures. In response to the partial lifting NATO removed some of the bilateral sanctions and began negotiations to reschedule Poland's debt.

Notes

[1] Aloysius Balawyder, *In the Clutches of the Kremlin, Canadian-East European Relations,* 1945-1962 Columbia University Press, 2000.

[2] *Ibid,* p.38.

[3] George Ignatieff, to the secretary of state for External Affairs, (hereafter referred as SSEA), DEA file 50165-40, National Archives of Canada, (hereafter noted as NAC).

[4] Imer Kovacs, "The Establishment in Hungary," in Lyman H. Legters, *Eastern Europe, Transformation and Revolution, 1945-199,* D.C. Heath and Company, Toronto, p. 169.

[5] N.A. Bulganin reply to the letter of Louis St. Laurent, November 26, 1946 in *Statements and Speeches,* DEA files NAC.

[6] Ivan Svitak, "Before the Occupation: Political Crisis in Czechoslovakia," in *Eastern Europe, op. cit.,* pp. 206-208.

[7] "2000 Words" A Statement on Democratization. Found in *Eastern Europe, ibid.,* pp. 211-217.

[8] See H. Gordon Skilling, *Czechoslovakia's Interrupted Revolution,* Princeton University Press, 1976 and Kurt Weiskopf, *The Agony of Czechoslovakia,* 36/38, Elk, London, England.

[9] *The Canadian Annual Review,* edited by John Saywell, University of Toronto, Press.

[10] *Ibid.*

[11] *Ibid.*

[12] *Ibid.*

[13] Canada, *Debates of the House of Commons,* October 17, 1968, Ottawa, pp. 1467-1468.

[14] For a summary of Polish survival history see Chapter I, "Roots of the Present", in M.K. Dziewanowski's book, *Poland in the 20th Century,* Columbia University Press, 1977, pp. 1-30.

[15] Andrzej Korbanski, "Poland" printed in *Communism in Eastern Europe,* edited by Teresa Rakowska-Harmstone and Andrew Gyorgy, Indiana University Press, 1979, pp. 40-41.

[16] Dziewanowski, *Poland in the 20th Century, op. cit.* p. 207.

[17] Adam Bromke, *Poland, The Last Decade,* Mosaic Press, Oakville, Ontario, 1981, see Chapters IV, Vand VI which deal with Gierek's tenure in office.

[18] *Ibid.*

[19] The twenty-one demands were presented to the Polish government on August 23, 1980. These demands are quoted in Lyman H. Legters (e) *Eastern Europe, op. cit.,* pp. 253-254.

[20] *The Canadian Annual Review of Politics and Public Affairs,* University of Toronto Press, 1981, p. 292.

[21] Trudeau's remarks to Bruce Phillips on December 21, 1981 were on the year-end interview.

[22] The Conservative members who took part in the debate were Joe Clark, leader of the opposition, Flora MacDonald, Eugene Paproski, John Crosby and Ron Stewart. Among of the Liberal members participating were Mark McGuigan, Pierre Trudeau and Jessie Fils.

[23] Mark McGuigan's address to the Fifth Session at the Follow-up Meeting of the CSCE, *Statements and Speeches,* February 9, 1982.

IV. INTERNATIONAL CLAIMS

Apart from the Polish Art Treasures saga that dragged from 1946 to 1960 no other issue affected Canada's relations with Eastern Europe more than the international claims. Trade was stifled by this problem and so were diplomatic and cultural relations. Ethnic communities pressured Ottawa to assist them in recovering some of their losses due to war and nationalization of property by the communist regimes. According to International Law the Canadian government had an obligation and the right to intervene on behalf of her citizens using both diplomatic and judicial procedures to ensure that just treatment was meted out.[1]

Unlike the United States and Switzerland, Canada was rather late in alerting her citizens of East European origin to the possibility of compensation. The main reason for her tardiness was the lack of effective levers to put pressure on communist regimes.[2] Her trade with Eastern Europe was relatively small in the early years of the Cold War and secondly, she did not possess large blocked funds belonging to East European countries, funds which could be used as effective levers.

The procedure for negotiation of international claims followed a certain pattern.[3] Canada had to come to an agreement in principle with the foreign country indicating a willingness to engage in such negotiations. Secondly, the government of Canada invited Canadian nationals to detail their claims, and then scrutinized them as to their reliability and their appropriateness. In the third stage, Canadian and foreign representatives met to discuss the submitted claims. The fourth step finalized the number of claims to be considered and stipulated the manner to be used in the settlement of the claims. The final step was left to the appointed Foreign Claims Commissioner who executed the recommendations of the "ad hoc committee."

The Czechoslovakian Claims

Out of the six East European countries, Poland and Czechoslovakia and their nationals submitted the largest number of claims. Poland was hamstrung by the detention of the Polish Art Treasures that were brought during the war to Canada for safekeeping. Czechoslovaks did not have a comparable hurdle to derail their attempt to resolve the issue of claims. However, there were other problems.

The Czechoslovak government refused to compensate nationals who became Canadian citizens after September 1938.[4] When the democratically elected government of Edward Benes assumed power in 1946 the properties of Nazi sympathizers were confiscated. In February 1948 communists under Klement Gottwald carried out a *coup* and formed a government. After seizing power the regime nationalized public property but left open the possibility of compensation for former owners.

In 1953, Canada reminded Czechoslovakia that her invitation to discuss claims remained unchanged even though Prague did not give any reply to the Canadian note of 1949. It is not surprising to have such a reaction during the height of the Cold War. The department of External Affairs had on file 470 claims amounting to $225,000,000 and the Canadian Custodian of the Enemy held $502,000 worth of Czechoslovak assets.[5] Thomas Bata, a shoe manufacturer, submitted a claim of $90,000,000. After close scrutiny the Canadian government through its legation in Prague submitted in 1952 a revised version. Now, there were only 140 claims amounting to $70 to $80 million instead of $225 million a situation created by the nationalization of property.[6]

The Czechoslovak government wanted to link the settlement of the claims with a trade agreement enabling the Prague government to pay some of the claims using trade transactions. Canada did not accept this suggestion, arguing that such an arrangement was contrary to the established trade policies.[7] Both Canada and Poland enjoyed MFN tariff treatment already permitting them freedom from quantitative restrictions of goods entering Canada. Unhappy with Canada's reply Czechoslovakia tried to weasel a concession. It suggested that the assets of $500,000 held by the Custodian of the Enemy be handed over to the Czech government and not to the former owners. After seeking advice from the departments of Justice and Finance and considering the approach the United States had taken towards her claims, the Canadian cabinet decided to retain the assets as a bargaining chip for concessions.

The Czechoslovak regime firmly dug its heels in and refused to budge from its original position. Canada's relations with Czechoslovakia remained rather tense after 1948. Efforts to engage Prague in a meaningful dialogue were suspended as an impasse was reached. The invasion of Czechoslovakia in 1968 by the Soviet Union further delayed the process of negotiations. The stalemate was finally broken when Canada gave a tacit recognition of the Czechoslovak nationalization law following the example of the United Kingdom and the United States who permitted the issue of claims to be tied to trade. In 1973 after twenty-five years of negotiations Canada and Czechoslovakia concluded the protracted negotiations and signed an agreement.[8]

Poland and the Claims Settlement

Although the claims of Czechoslovakia and Poland were linked together by the department of External Affairs, there were particular problems affecting each of the countries. For example, Czechoslovakia had more hard currency than did Poland. The former was able to sell her products in the Western markets more readily than the latter. Polish officials even spoke of giving Canada, if that was agreeable, coal as a means of settling claims. Canada vigorously resisted such bilateral trade settlement of claims. Unlike the Czechoslovaks Canadian Poles submitted informal claim requests directly to the Polish government.

The major obstacle to any dialogue of claims settlement was the issue of the Polish Art Treasures that were brought to Canada in 1940 for safekeeping. For a number of internal and external reasons these treasures were detained in Canada against the will of the Canadian government. Once they were returned to Poland in 1960 the avenue was open for a meaningful dialogue on the issue of claims.[9]

As in the case of Czechoslovakia, the Canadian government issued a call to Canadian citizens to list and describe their land and other properties that were nationalized by the Polish government. One of the difficulties encountered by Polish nationals was the scarcity of authentic documentation. Property deeds and legal papers were destroyed during World War II and therefore oral testimonies were often used in lieu of documents

The first meeting of Polish and Canadian delegations took place in October of 1968. At this preliminary meeting various types of claims were discussed as well as "cut-off dates" of eligibility for the submission of claims. Altogether Polish Canadians submitted 600 claims against Poland valued at 41 million dollars.[10] At the outset 217 claims were rejected on the for lack of evidence to vouch for the nationality of the claimants. It was agreed that the claimant had to be a Canadian citizen, either by birth or by naturalization, before the nationalization of property took place. The adjusted value of claims was reduced to $26 million dollars and then again further reduced to the amount that reflected the current value of the property. The extent of leverage of the said property affected its price. Polish Canadians did not have the leverage that the Czechoslovaks enjoyed, for the Canadian-Polish import-export trade was rather small.[11]

Ottawa attempted to get Poland re-activated in the solution of the claims by suggesting that some of the $209, 300 assets held by the custodian would be set free if, in turn, "block bank accounts" held by the Polish government would likewise be released.[12] This "tit for tat" approach brought a response; negotiations were resumed.

Now the issue that stalled the process was the authenticity of the documents. The Polish government insisted that each claim be supported by evidence of a legal title or other records. Upon receiving this evidence the Polish authorities examined the information submitted by the claimants and in many cases demanded affidavits to substantiate their claims. This procedure was time consuming and open to manipulation. Generally, it was difficult for Polish Canadians to get information on their property in Poland. To further complicate matters Polish authorities imposed arbitrary taxes and penalties on foreign property.

Despite the desire on the part of Canada and Poland to have the claims settlement end in a satisfactory conclusion other issues appeared on the horizon impeding this objective. Poland wanted to establish a consulate in Toronto in order to have contact with the large Polish community and to open an office in Halifax in order to service the Polish fishing fleet. Canada considered these two requests unacceptable for two main reasons; first, these concessions would require added supervision of the Polish government officials some of whom could be spies and secondly, the Polish Canadian community, most of whom were anti-communist, would object to this concession. However, Canada was delighted to finally discover a leverage that could be used to expedite the claims issue. Canada revisited the Polish suggestion and agreed to permit Poland to have her consulate in Toronto and to reconsider the issue of an office in Halifax if and when the Polish government resumed the claims negotiation.

In October 1971 a Polish delegation led by Marian Krzak,[13] the Polish vice-minister of finance, met with Mitchell Sharp, the Canadian secretary of state for External Affairs, and concluded an agreement providing a lump sum of $1.225 million dollars to be paid to the claimants. Poland opened a trade office in Halifax in 1971 and a consulate in Toronto in 1977.

Four Other East European Countries

(A) Yugoslavia

Although Czechoslovakia and Poland were the largest claimants with whom Canada negotiated, other Eastern bloc countries submitted their claims and agreed to arrangements similar to those concluded with Czechoslovakia and Poland. On December 23, 1949 the United Kingdom and Yugoslavia reached an understanding of a settlement of claims of British nationals whose property was nationalized by Tito's regime. Under the broad definition, British nationals were all citizens of the Commonwealth including Canadians.

The department of External Affairs advertised this arrangement in the *Canada Gazette* and contacted many Canadian citizens. A Canadian representative was present when the claims were examined. To be eligible one had to be a Canadian or a British subject at the time of seizure of property on January 1, 1949. The claimants had until October 1, 1954 to present their claims.

A Foreign Compensation Commission examined 141 Canadian claims, dismissing 47 of these and awarding three million pounds sterling to 94 claimants. Since the original cut off date, other claims were filed taking advantage of new nationalization measures. The majorities of claimants were not Canadian citizens and therefore were unable to benefit from the agreement of 1949. The Yugoslav government pointed out to Canadian negotiators that Yugoslavia suffered much from the horrors of World War II and therefore should not be assessed a heavy indemnity. Not having hard currency Yugoslav officials suggested that in lieu of money services and land for the Canadian legation building could be one means of settling the Canadian claims. Canada agreed to this proposal. However, as late as 1983 Canada and Yugoslavia continued to discuss new claims arising from new laws on nationalization of property.

(B) Hungary

Unlike Poland and Czechoslovakia there were relatively few Hungarian, Rumanian and Bulgarian claimants who enquired about the property that was nationalized by the communist regimes. The Canadian government placed claims on record but did not engage in any bargaining as she did not do in the case of Poland nor did she analyze the nature and the value of the claims. Ottawa had on record the pre-World War II debts called "the Massey-Harris" claim of $700,000, war damage claim of about $187,000 for which Hungary was liable under the Paris Peace Treaty of 1947 and the nationalization claims, particularly the Bata claim of about two and half million dollars for the nationalized shoe factory. Canada authorized the assets of $150, 692 to be used by Hungary as a compensation for the claims.[14]

Since Canada did not have her own embassy in Hungary all requests were channeled through the British embassy in Budapest. Unfortunately, during and after the Hungarian revolution of 1956, the British burned some of the claim files. However, the Hungarian government was willing to arrive at a settlement by putting forward a "package deal," which stipulated a number of conditions. Hungary was willing to reach an agreement on debts and claims by releasing "blocked Hungarian assets" if Canada, on her part, would allow Hungary to open a consular office in Ottawa. The Canadian government agreed to the first request but left the issue of a consular office in abeyance. Later the Cabinet approved the release of Hungarian and Romanian assets with the understanding that the remainder of the assets would be applied towards war claims.

(C) Romania

As in the case of Hungary so in the case of Romania, Canada had the right, under the Paris Peace Treaty of 1947 to confiscate the assets formerly owned by Romania but vested in the Canadian custodian.[15] Canada was entitled to apply such assets towards the satisfactory solution of her claims and those of her citizens who lost property during the Second World War or had their property nationalized.

Although no war claims against Romania were found eligible she did have other obligations under the Peace Treaty. Canada had substantial claims for defaulted interest by the Romanian government on bonds. The three East European countries, Hungary, Romania and Bulgaria were interested in negotiating trade agreements with Canada and in establishing diplomatic relations. Following a satisfactory settlement of the claims a resident ambassador was appointed to Hungary and to Romania in 1975.

(D) Bulgaria

With Bulgaria a number of factors were responsible for expediting bilateral relations with Canada. By 1966 the custodian had already released

$90,428 worth of Bulgarian assets seized during World War II leaving only $7,025 to be dispersed among claimants who did not have an opportunity to avail themselves of the assets.[16] As to the outstanding claims, the Canadian government accepted the Bulgarian offer of $40,000 as a lump-sum settlement. The Canadian government was disappointed when she learned that the Bata claims were considered ineligible for compensation.[17]

Another issue crept up in the discussion of war claims. Bulgaria, Romania and Hungary argued that they should be compensated on the grounds that the Nazis persecuted them. The Canadian government, however, dismissed these claims, noting that the Peace Treaties that Canada had signed did not specify such a provision.

Notes

[1] See the pamphlet issued by the Permanent Court of International Justice, Series A, no. 2, p.12, 1924, NAC.

[2] Donald MacDonald, "Canada's Recent Experience in International Claims", *Statement and Speeches,* Department of External Affairs, (hereafter noted as DEA, National Archives of Canada (hereafter noted as NAC).

[3] *Ibid.*

[4] Memorandum of Secretary of State for External Affairs (hereafter as SSEA). June 17, 1949, RG 25, ACC 83-84/1233(2) Box 42, File 614-G.

[5] *Ibid.*

[6] "Canadian Claims against Czechoslovakia" Annex 'A', A memorandum for the Minister, October 29, 1963, DEA File 912-913, NAC.

[7] "Canadian Nationalization Claims Against Eastern Europe", June 26, 1963, *ibid.*

[8] *Canada Annual Report,* 1973, Department for External Affairs, Ottawa.

[9] Aloysius Balawyder, *The Odyssey of the Polish Treasures,* St. Francis Xavier University Press, 1978.

[10] Memorandum to the Cabinet, "Canadian Claims against Poland", March 27, 1969, RG 20 vol. 2626, file 20.

[11] *Ibid.*

[12] *Ibid.*

[13] *Canadian Annual Report.* 1971.

[14] "Canadian Claims against Hungary, Romania, Bulgaria and the USSR" Annex "D," DEA, RG 25, box 5284, file 9152-40, NAC.

[15] "Memorandum to the Cabinet," July 20, 1960, *ibid.*

[16] To the deputy minister of Finance from USSEA, May 18, 1966, RG 20, box 1978, file 20-321-1315, DEA files, NAC.

[17] *Ibid.*

V. AN UNEASY DÉTENTE

Canada's foreign policy was focused on peace and stability in the world. Canada worked tirelessly to make the United Nations an effective institution for preserving world peace by lessening tensions between East and West. Canadian diplomats assisted in drawing up the Universal Charter of Rights and participated in peace-keeping missions in Indo-China, Nigeria, Palestine and Cyprus. As a member of the North Atlantic Treaty Organization, Canada emphasized the importance of the non-military aspects as stated in Article 2 of the Treaty. In the 1970's she was an active member in the formulation of the Helsinki Accords.

Canada fully realized that the Soviet Union would not permit her satellites to leave the Warsaw Pact Alliance. Canada wanted to prevent any conflagration between the two military alliances. Her strategy was a positive one; every effort was to be exercised to present Canada as a country of peace and prosperity and have this presentation open to some possibilities. The programs of the CBC-IS beamed to Eastern Europe aimed to promote closer relations with the Soviet Union and her satellites. Ottawa insisted that the portrayal of Canada and the Canadian daily life over the CBC-IS should be reliable, balanced and objective. At no time were the broadcasts aimed to stir up emotions of antagonism and fear. The spirit of détente underscored the importance of building confidence and trust between the governments of the East and West and the peoples of each of the two camps. The guiding principle was to lessen tensions between the two blocs, tensions that prevented a frank and honest dialogue.

The generally-agreed time frame of détente stretched from the resolution of the Cuban crisis of 1962 to the demise of the Soviet control of Eastern Europe in 1990. Between these two dates there were events, which indicated that all tensions could lead to confrontation. At times it appeared that the remnants of the Cold War continued to linger on. In 1968 the Warsaw Pact countries led by the Soviet Union invaded Czechoslovakia, stifling the on-going democratic reforms. Eleven years later the Soviet Union invaded Afghanistan and in 1981 the Polish government declared martial law, outlawed the Solidarity and dampened economic, social and political reforms.

The movement initiated by the Helsinki Accords offered the people of Eastern Europe many opportunities they did not enjoy before. The violations of human rights were carefully monitored and made public. Some of the Soviet-bloc countries were named culprits of such violations. The movement of peoples, be they tourists or immigrants, from Eastern Europe to the West was encouraged and scores of government officials and bureaucrats from both sides exchanged visits. Scientific, cultural and academic exchanges multiplied as the people from both the East and the West attempted to appreciate one another's culture.

Definitions of Détente

The meaning of the word "détente" varied according to the ideology and values of individuals or groups. Although the terminology of definition also varied among Western observers, yet most of them agreed that "détente" was an understanding leading to peace. Some advocates of East-West détente called it "relative normalcy" or "new structure of peace." Others labeled détente as a "relaxation" of tensions.[1] The last mentioned definition was the one Canada agreed upon. Mark MacGuigan, secretary of state for External Affairs at the opening session of the North Atlantic Ministerial Meeting held in Luxembourg on May 17, 1982, considered détente as a lessening of tensions between the East and the West with tangible benefits resulting in the increase of trade, human contacts, family reunifications and human rights.[2]

In contrast, the elaboration of the Western definition was markedly different from that of the Soviet Union. From Moscow's point of view "détente" was essentially an ideological struggle, short of war whose main aim was to obtain the "maximum benefits from "co-operation with the West ...particularly in obtaining access to western technology and credits." [3] Nikita Khrushchev at the 20th Congress of the Communist Party of the Soviet Union introduced the word "peaceful co-existence" which to him was "détente." Although he dismissed the possibility of an armed conflict with the West, he encouraged a peaceful "socialist and communist" conquest of the world. [4]

As experience has shown détente was a beginning of something bigger and more significant than the various definitions seem to indicate. International peace was at stake. Following the Soviet-led invasion of Czechoslovakia the Warsaw Treaty Organization and the North Atlantic Treaty Organization became aware of the danger of an escalated armed race and increased tensions between the West and the East. The Soviet Union took the initiative in suggesting a conference on Security and Co-operation in Europe (CSCE). The Soviet Union had a hidden agenda for she wanted the West to accept the existing boundaries and political changes made by the Yalta Conference in 1945.[5] In turn the West pushed for a program of freedom of movement of peoples, increased human contacts and family reunifications as well as for economic, cultural and technological exchanges.

The issues for discussion required compromise, diplomatic dexterity and plenty of patience. Canadians of East European descent did not favour any legitimization of boundaries and governments imposed on them by the Soviet Union. At the same time they realized that many benefits could result from an agreement between the East and the West.

The negotiators were fully aware of the need of a "confidence building" mechanism before meaningful negotiations could take place. In 1971 an agreement was signed permitting unhindered access to West Berlin. In May 1972 President Richard Nixon and Leonid Brezhnev met and discussed disarmament. As a result of this meeting the Strategic Arms Limitation Treaty (SALT) came about. Canada was pleased with the continuing progress that had been made but felt that the Mutual and Balanced Force reduction (MBFR) and the CSCE should be kept separate and moving forward in parallel pattern.[6]

CSCE Discussions

The CSCE discussions began in Helsinki in November 1972 and continued until 1975. Canada as well as East European countries were actively involved in these discussions. The first Helsinki talks centered on the guiding principles that should govern negotiations. The Warsaw Pact countries argued that the subject of the use of force and the threat of war should occupy the first place in the preliminary discussions on peace and security. In addition, they argued that the existing boundaries should be recognized as inviolable. NATO countries agreed to the existing *de facto* recognition but stopped short of granting a *de jure* recognition as a sign of respect for the wishes of East Europeans.[7]

The second round of talks took place in Geneva. Again East Europeans and Canadians were actively involved. Altogether there were 35 countries represented. The main objective of this session was to flesh out the enunciated principles, making them relevant. The mere logistics necessary to reach a consensus were at times overwhelming. Added to the existing detailed work the persecution of Soviet scientist Andrei Sakharov and the world-renowned writer Alexander Solzhenitsyn were singled out as problems that needed immediate attention.[8] At this round Canada and Denmark were given the responsibility of encouraging human contacts and family reunifications contained in Basket Three of the Accords. Human rights and freedoms were also included within the jurisdiction of these two countries.

The Final Act of the Helsinki Accords

The final act of the accords consisted in the signing of the document by the heads of state. Thirty-five heads of state gave their assent to the agreement. Canada and each of the six East European states as well as the Soviet Union signed the Agreement. This document was an outstanding landmark in the quest for security and co-operation. It was not a treaty nor did it endorse the Soviet Union's hegemony in Eastern Europe; rather it emphasized equality of all states, upheld territorial integrity and provided peaceful means of settling disputes. By stressing non-interference in the internal affairs of each country it gave Eastern Europe a sense of hope and stability.[9]

Evaluation and Implementation

The signatories of the Helsinki Accords vied with each other, promising to put into effect the principles of the agreement. But even before the ink was dry on the signed document some of the countries ignored the promises they had made to respect the human rights of all people no matter where they were found. The framers of the Accords wisely inserted a means of reminding the offenders of their promises. Periodic reviews were required to assure the implementation of the Accords. The first of these review conferences took place in Belgrade from October 4, 1977 to March 8, 1978.

Secluded behind closed doors 400 representatives from 35 countries heard a litany of violations of the Helsinki Agreement. Some representatives did not agree with the allegations and said so. Not only were the negative remarks refuted in no uncertain terms but also the usefulness of the exercise was questioned. The Soviet bloc countries gave the review conference a failing mark. The European Economic Community and NATO with the exception of France, who did not wish to be included with the European countries, recognized that some significant progress was made in respect to human rights and freedoms.[10] At the same time they pointed out that there were violations of the ten principles governing the Accords.

Canada, France, Belgium and West Germany made a 180-degree about turn when they at first were silent and more or less oblivious of the violations of human rights in the Soviet Union and her satellites and then changed their minds condemning the Soviet bloc countries for their violation of human rights. The catalyst that prompted this change was the dramatic disclosure of the show trials in Czechoslovakia and the arrest of Soviet dissidents. Before dispersing, all the delegates agreed to continue monitoring violations of the Helsinki Accords and reporting them at the Madrid Conference.[11]

Right from its very beginning the atmosphere at the Madrid Conference was charged with suspicion and distrust. The Soviet Union was considered a violator of the Helsinki Accords because of her invasion of Afghanistan in 1979 and her role in Polish affairs leading to the imposition of martial law in 1981. For three years (1980-1983) the participants wrangled and wrangled with one another, accusing each other of duplicity and disloyalty.

At the opening of the Conference held in Madrid in 1980, Mark MacGuigan, pointed out that the Soviet invasion of Afghanistan caused irreparable damage to détente. "At a minimum," he said, "Soviet actions have challenged directly the principles in the Final Act of sovereign equality refraining from the threat or the use of force, inviolability of frontiers, territorial integrity of states…and self -determination of peoples…." [12]

In concert with her NATO partners Canada imposed sanctions on the Soviet Union. Grain sales were restricted, academic, scientific and cultural exchanges were suspended, the Moscow Olympic games were boycotted, Soviet Aeroflot's flights to and from Canada were restricted and credits to the Soviet Union were frozen.[13]

In contrast, Canadian sanctions on Poland for imposing martial law and outlawing Solidarity were less severe than those imposed on the Soviet Union when the latter invaded Afghanistan. NATO knew that the real culprit responsible in the violation of human rights and freedoms was the Soviet Union who influenced the Polish government to impose martial law. Canada continued to ship grain to Poland, provided Poland an additional $500 million dollars of credit, allocated 20,000 tonnes of fish and rescheduled the 1981 debt payments.[14] In addition, Canadians of Polish extraction sent food to the people of Poland. Although martial law was lifted in July 1983, NATO maintained its sanctions because Poland introduced new measures of repression equivalent to those enacted by the martial law.

Despite the setbacks affecting détente the flame of freedom and openness continued to shine. The newly-elected member of the Politburo, Mikhail Gorbachev,[15] showed indications of a new vision for the Soviet Union. His numerous trips to Western Europe, the United States and Canada convinced him that the West did not intend to revive the Cold War. On the contrary, he discovered that the people in the West had fears, joys and aspirations similar to those living in the Soviet Union and in Eastern Europe. He firmly believed that meaningful détente could bring unity and peace to the divided world.

Gorbachev coined two terms that suggested his program: "glasnost" (openness) and "perestroika" (reconstruction). He argued that the Soviet people and the satellites required freedom to be creative and productive. At the same time, in his opinion, there was a considerable amount of work needed to "rebuild" the existing society. The appearance of Gorbachev on the Soviet scene at this time was good news to the people behind the "iron curtain." But at the same time they realized that no substantial change in their country could take place without the support and blessing of the Soviet Union. Having Gorbachev at the helm of Soviet Union augured for the possibility of reforms and freedom not only in the Soviet Union but also in Eastern Europe.

The satellite states were reliable barometers for measuring some aspects of these changes. By 1986 Poland, Yugoslavia and Hungary enjoyed a considerable degree of freedom. Ministerial, diplomatic and government visits increased considerably. Trade expanded and so did cultural and scientific exchanges. A considerable amount of movement of peoples occurred during the détente. Hundreds of citizens from every East European state applied to visit their relatives in Canada and the United States. Some were even permitted to immigrate to Canada and other countries. At last the Helsinki Accords began to show some tangible results.

The last CSCE conference was held in Vienna, beginning on January 10, 1989. The atmosphere of freedom and independence was evident at this gathering. The delegates renewed their promises to observe the principles of the Accords and to work incessantly for human rights, for freedom of religion, freedom from arbitrary arrest, detention or exile; the right to move from one country to another; the right to publish and the right to exchange information. A new dawn had finally come to Eastern Europe.

Notes

[1] Stanislav J. Kirschbaum, "Twelve Months after Helsinki: a Debate Rages over Détente," *International Perspective,* 1976, May/June. pp. 34-35.

[2] Mark McGuigan, "Atlantic Alliance dedicated to the preservation of peace," *Statements & Speeches,* May 17, 1982, Department of External Affairs, (hereafter noted as DEA).

[3] *Ibid.*

[4] Adam Bromke & Derek Novak, editors, "Introduction," *The Communist States in the Era of Détente, 1971-1977,* Mosaic Press, 1977, p. 2.

[5] Karl E. Birnbaum, *Peace in Europe: East-West Relations, 1966-1969 and Prospects for European Settlement,* London, Oxford University Press, 1970.

[6] Donald Page, "High Hopes and Disappointing Realities," found in Aloysius Balawyder, (ed) *Canadian-Soviet Relations, 1939-1980,* Mosaic Press, Toronto, 1981, pp. 66-67.

[7] *Ibid.* pp. 67-68.

[8] *Ibid.* pp. 70-71.

[9] *Ibid.* p. 73.

[10] H. Gordon Skilling, "Belgrade and Human Rights; Success or Failure," *International Perspective,* DEA, Ottawa, 1978, p. 19. See also David Matas, "Helsinki Watch in Budapest" *International Perspective,* January-February, 1986 DEA, pp. 3-6.

[11] *Ibid.* p.20.

[12] R.B. Byers (ed), *The Canadian Annual Review of Politics and Public Affairs, 1980-1981, NAC* Ottawa.

[13] *The Canadian Annual Review, 1980,* DEA, p. 51.

[14] *The Canadian Annual Review, 1981,* DEA, p. 80.

[15] Robert G. Kaiser, *Why Gorbachev Happened,* Simon & Schuster, New York, 1992. An interesting and valuable account of the achievements and failures of Gorbachev.

VI. BILATERAL RELATIONS

Relations between Canada and East European countries were bilateral and multilateral. Relations like trade, claims, and cultural, academic and scientific exchanges were more appropriate in the multilateral category whereas fisheries, ship-jumping, consular problems and pulp and paper projects seemed to belong better in the bilateral sphere. In some cases the differences between one category and the other were so slight that they could be in either category.

Canadian-Polish Relations

Bilateral relations between Canada and Poland were substantially greater than with any other East European country. Government documents clearly indicate the extent of these relations particularly during the period of détente. Poland was the favorite East European country with whom Canada developed relations. Apart from the Ukrainian Canadians, Polish ethnic Canadians formed the largest Slavic group in Canada.

Despite the imposed communist regime in Poland, the two countries cultivated correct relations with one another. The Polish Art Treasures controversy was a "thorn in the side" in these relations until it was solved in 1960. The wonderful co-operation between Poland and Canada during World War II was deeply ingrained in the minds and hearts of Canadians and Poles. Following the war the two countries found themselves in peacekeeping assignments in Indo-China, Palestine and Angola. Officially Canadians and Poles were on opposite sides, with the Poles representing the Soviet bloc and the Canadians the West, but on the nonofficial level they were friends. There is one aspect they shared namely under the shadow of their powerful neighbours, the Soviet Union and the United States.

Polish Seamen Jumping Ships

Besides the lingering irritation created by the unsolved international claims, ship jumping was one of the other issues that soured bilateral relations during the period 1963-1990. Ship-jumping consisted of a fishing crew leaving their boats and seeking asylum in another country: a practice used by some East Europeans, particularly Yugoslavs and Poles. According to Canadian law anyone who could provide evidence that he/she would be prosecuted or persecuted upon return to one's country could apply for a landed immigrant status. The immigrant would then appear before the Immigration Appeal Board, which decided whether the landed immigrant status should be granted. If the Board refused to grant this status the immigrant could request the Minister of Manpower and Immigration to review the case.

The Polish government found this procedure unsatisfactory. The Polish ambassador[1] to Canada argued that the "jumping" seamen should be sent back to Poland as Canada had done to the 350 Greek and Yugoslav seamen who "jumped the ships." He claimed that the Polish ethnic community in Canada helped these seamen by harbouring them, providing them money and promising help them to find employment. The Canadian government denied these allegations.

The Canadian government pointed out to the Polish ambassador that the deportation of seamen was not in the hands of the government but rather in the hands of the Immigration Appeal Board, a quasi-judicial body that made recommendations to the government.[2] In addition Ottawa refuted the claim that the seamen were encouraged to jump ship. Canadian officials also contended that the seamen were not captives of the government but were free to talk to anyone they met and to walk anywhere in the city of Halifax while awaiting the results of the Board. Being unable to attend meetings of the Board frustrated the Polish consul. However, the consul was aware that he could meet with the seamen in the presence of an interpreter, an immigration officer and a RCMP officer.

At the same time the Polish authorities appraised the Canadian government of the consequences of not having the full complement of seamen to operate the ships and the effect of not having. qualified workers.[3] The sensitive issue was raised at a meeting held in Ottawa on October 12, 1970 between Mitchell Sharp, the Canadian secretary of state for External Affairs, and the Polish foreign minister, Stefan Jedrychowski. The foreign minister repeated the allegations of some of the other members of the Polish legation who claimed that the seamen were "encouraged by groups," presumably Polish Canadians, to desert their ships. He accused the department of Manpower and Immigration of preventing these deserters from being deported.[4]

Sharp responded that anyone who enters Canada legally or illegally could apply for immigrant status. Furthermore, if these new immigrants did not wish to be deported they had the option of appealing to the Appeal Board. Finally he emphasized that it was against Canadian law to encourage seamen to defect.[5]

On April 21,1971 the Immigration Detention Centre in Halifax was closed and the Polish "ship jumpers" were sent to Quebec City where they under-went a process of questionings carried out by the Immigration Board of Inquiry. The move of the Detention Centre to Quebec City was aimed to prevent any interference from Polish community in the investigation of the "ship jumpers".

The discussions between the Polish and Canadian officials as well as the change to the Quebec Detention Centre did not terminate "ship jumping." But something else did. The implementation of the Helsinki Accords made it possible for Polish tourists and visitors to legally stay in Canada for a period of six months during which time they could receive monetary help and work to defray their expenses. By 1987 the policy of family reunification was accepted by Poland and Hungary. Now some of the seamen were not only permitted to remain in Canada as landed immigrants but also to bring their family over.

Issues Related to Ship-Jumping

Obviously Poland was anxious to solve the problem of "ship-jumping" and offered a solution. The Polish government suggested that an establishment of an office[7] in Halifax would be an important step towards the solution of this problem. In addition such an office would eliminate the necessity of hiring agents to negotiate fishing arrangements and thus save Poland millions of dollars. Canada appreciated the Polish suggestion and felt that this item could be brought forward as leverage in the solution of the claims dispute.

There were other issues the Poles wished to address. They wanted to establish a trade office in Toronto and have Polish personnel stationed at Dalimpex, a Canadian-registered company owned by one of the Polish export corporations opened in 1965.[8] Canada was wary about this request for two reasons. The Canadian authorities and the RCMP argued that the new office could provide the Polish government with another avenue to obtain confidential information on Canada. In addition the Polish communist regime might try to influence the Polish ethnic community.

Time and again the Canadian government harboured fears that an expansion of any East European legations might increase an opportunity of espionage. The Igor Gouzenko saga of espionage was always in the minds of the Canadian security agency. Multiplication of East European trade and diplomatic posts required increased security and personnel.

After prolonged negotiations Poland received what she wanted when she and Canada signed on October 15, 1971, a claims agreement that granted a trade office in Halifax where the Polish personnel could work closely with the Polish shipping company. Poland was also permitted to open a consulate in Toronto, a city where the majority of Polish Canadians lived. These concessions also helped some Canadians. The consulate made it easier for Canadians to get necessary information on family reunification and to arrange trips to Poland. In addition, these facilities provided Canadian and Polish trade commissioners, businessmen, technicians and government officials easier access to useful information.

Kwidzin Pulp and Paper Mill

The Helsinki Accords encouraged international investments. For some time H.A. Simons Company had expressed interest in investing in Eastern Europe. The Company realized that the labour costs were much lower in Poland than they were in Canada. After many meetings the company agreed, in principle, to build a bleached draft mill, a semi-chemical pulp mill and a paper mill in Kwidzyn Poland. The Canadian government through the Export Development Corporation assisted Simons by lending it money. In 1976 Canada signed an eighty-million dollar contract with Poland agreeing to supply the necessary machinery for the project. Canada also provided the technical and engineering expertise.[9] This international experiment proved successful and a similar arrangement was made between Simons Company, Czechoslovakia and Canada.

Fisheries and Canadian-Polish Relations

Other agreements were signed. Poland and Canada signed important treaties governing fishing zones. In 1977 the Canadian fishing zones were extended from 12 miles to 200 miles both in the Atlantic and Pacific Oceans. The following year Canada signed bilateral agreements with Norway, Portugal, Spain, the USSR, Poland, Bulgaria, and Romania.[10] According to these agreements Canada permitted foreign vessels to fish in Canadian waters provided they possessed appropriate licenses.

In 1978 also Canada joined six other nations and signed a Convention on Future Multilateral Co-operation in the Northwest Atlantic Fisheries. This Convention was responsible for the creation of NAFO (Northwest Atlantic Fisheries Organization) whose prime objective was to provide guidance for the management of fishing beyond the 200-mile limit.[11]

It was one thing to sign treaties and conventions, but it was another matter to have the parties adhere to their terms. Canada complained on a number of occasions that the bilateral fishing agreements were not fully adhered to. According to Canadian officials some of the Polish fishing boats did not have licenses and did not buy sufficient Canadian fish products as stated in the agreement.[12] Over-fishing was another issue brought to the attention of the Polish foreign minister, Jerzy Jedrychowski who paid an official visit to Canada in October 1970. The minister refuted this allegation claiming that Poland carefully and faithfully followed the rules of the Convention.

Family Reunification

Another bilateral issue was family reunification. During the Cold War there was virtually no immigration to Canada from Poland. Polish officials argued that every citizen was needed to help rebuild their war-torn country. Visas to travel abroad were difficult to obtain. Canada did not help matters for she carefully screened visitors from East European countries in an attempt to prevent communist agitators from entering the country.

With the coming of détente the Canadian embassy in Warsaw was inundated with requests from Poles who wished to visit or to immigrate to Canada in order to join their relatives. The Canadian-Polish urged the Canadian government to make it easier for families to reunite. The president of the Congress, Casmir Bielski, pointed out that family separations caused untold distress to the parties concerned and in many cases led to divorces.[13] He asked the government to do its utmost to reunite families.

In late 1970s the Polish government began to assist relatives who wanted to be reunited. Some of the cases were made more difficult by Polish citizens' illegal entry into Canada. It was a round about way of immigrating to Canada. Generally speaking, the person would ask and receive authorization to visit a relative(s) in Canada but later decide to remain in Canada and apply for landed immigrant status.[14] Once the person received this status he/she could attempt to bring to Canada relatives by sponsoring them. Polish authorities were firmly against a such circuitous manner of leaving Poland. However, as far as the Canadian government was concerned this procedure was legal.

By the latter part of the 1970s a change began to occur. By signing the Helsinki Accords Poland agreed to a freer movement of people.[15] Taking the year 1975, as an example, 5,000 Poles visited Canada and some 1,000 immigrated to Canada. In 1977 there were difficult cases presented to the Polish authorities involving 174 persons, most of whom were resolved successfully.[16] In addition to the loosening of immigration laws, travel to and from Poland became easier.

Canadian-Yugoslav Relations

Yugoslavia was one of the three East European countries Canada resumed relations established during the War. The other two countries were Czechoslovakia and Poland. In each of these countries Canada opened legations to monitor what was happening in the Soviet-bloc states. During the Stalinist period and a decade afterwards there were little immigration, trade and exchanges between the East and the West. Countries that had a bit more freedom were Czechoslovakia (1946-48) and Yugoslavia after she broke away from the Soviet Union in 1949.[17]

This rupture was a sensitive one, for Tito did not want to antagonize Stalin too much. Although Yugoslavia withdrew from Comecon and the Warsaw Treaty Organization, she did not join the Western allies nor did she become an anti-communist state. Instead, she joined "non-aligned" states such as Egypt, India and Burma. Economically she adopted a "self-management" system.

No longer a member of the Cominform with whom she originally carried on trade and stricken by severe drought, Yugoslavia asked the West for help. This she received from the United States and the United Kingdom who sent food, medical supplies and consumer goods to Yugoslavia.[18] Canada contributed fish and money, the latter through the services of the United Nations International Children Fund.[19]

Canada's relations with Yugoslavia were rather uneven. Diplomatically Canada was happy that Yugoslavia broke away from Stalin's grip, but many Canadians, particularly Roman Catholics and Canadians of East European descent including members of parliament, considered Yugoslavia a communist state, a state that persecuted Christians and was governed by a communist dictator. This negative attitude was demonstrated when Tito's trip to the United States and Canada was postponed because of the strong objections from Christians notably Catholics and Slavic groups. Catholics were furious with the treatment that Cardinal Aloysius Stepinac had received at the hands of the Yugoslav authorities. He was accused of aiding Germans during the Second World War.[20]

Tito's visit to Canada took place from November 2 to 7, 1971, fourteen years after the first intended visit was cancelled. Accompanied by Madame Broz and the state secretary for Foreign Affairs he visited key cities in Canada. As a result of the visit scientific and technical contacts were negotiated between the Yugoslav and Canadian officials.[21] Furthermore, non-immigrant visas were not longer required to travel to Canada and trade between the two countries received a welcome boost.

Yugoslav Canadian Ethnic Communities

There were always differences among various Yugoslav ethnic groups caused by ideology, politics, history, cultural background and religion. Serbs and Croats did not get along with one another nor did Slovenes and Serbs. The Croats and Slovenes felt that the Serbs were over-bearing and domineering. Added to the existing nationalist rivalries there persisted a deep resentment of the communist regime. In many cases prejudice, distrust and rivalry were brought to Canada by the immigrants and were played out in Toronto and Ottawa.

On Yugoslav national days a charade of protest and nationalism was displayed on the streets of Toronto. Most of the marches and demonstrations, noisy as they were at times, were rather orderly. But on two occasions, in 1965 and 1967 explosions occurred in the vicinity of the Yugoslav consulate in Toronto.[22] No group declared itself responsible for these explosions but the

Toronto Metropolitan police felt that a radical Serbian Youth Movement of Freedom (SOPO) was the guilty party.

Another organization, the Ustachi, planned a series of demonstrations on the tenth anniversary of the independence of Croatia.[23] The Yugoslav ambassador was rather nervous, expecting the worse. The Toronto Metropolitan Police made it clear that neither violence nor disorder would be tolerated during the demonstration. To the surprise of all, Croatian nationalists peacefully paraded in front of the Yugoslav consulate in Toronto, displayed their placards and left. There were no demonstrations before the Yugoslav embassy in Ottawa.[24]

Despite the quiet demonstration, the Yugoslav ambassador felt uncomfortable and again contacted the department of External Affairs informing it of an alleged terrorist attack. The Canadian minister reassured the ambassador that the police in Ottawa and Toronto would provide the embassy the needed protection.[25] These incidents of terrorism and demonstrations convinced Ottawa that it would be unwise to open new Yugoslav offices in Canada.[26]

Canadian-Czechoslovak Relations

Canada established a legation in Prague in 1946. That same year elections were held and a coalition government was formed with Klement Gottwald chosen as prime minister. The communist party received 38 percent of the votes and therefore was given important cabinet posts: the office of prime minister, minister of the interior and agriculture. It was the only East European country that had a democratically and freely elected government. But two years later in 1948 the communist party orchestrated a *coup* and formed a communist government patterned on that of the Soviet Union.

Noticeable changes followed. Foreign newspapers were no longer displayed in the market place; travel restrictions were enforced; and listening to CBC International Service, the BBC, the Voice of America and the Radio Free Europe was a risky pastime. Communist informers were numerous who reported one to the government agents. Members of Western legations including Canadian were continuously harassed by the communist regime. Canada complained to the Czechoslovak government about the harassment but without any success.

Restrictions continued under the next communist leader, Antonin Novotny (1956-1968). However, there was a bright spot in his tenure of office that had a positive effect on Canada. Under his leadership Czechoslovakia participated in Montreal Expo, 1967, the hundredth anniversary of Canadian Confederation. The Czech pavilion was an interesting and creative display of Czechoslovakian history, traditions and contribution to world culture. Thousands of tourists lined up and waited for hours to see the interior of the pavilion and enjoy the concerts held there. Some 5,000 Czechoslovaks visited Expo including Novotny, Josef Lenart, and the prime minister.[27]

For those who were unable to travel to Canada to see Expo 67, the Canadian government used films, radio and television to introduce Canadian culture, art, literature, music and drama to the Czechoslovaks.[28] The sustained publicity made it possible for the Czech and Slovak people living in the remotest parts of the country to learn about Canada. In restaurants, in the cinemas, on the billboards, on television and on the radio Canada was presented in favourable light.

The following year Novotny was replaced by an open-minded secretary of the Communist Party, Alexander Dubcek, who attempted to the inaugurate a democratic government, the withdrawal of Soviet troops from Czechoslovakia, the termination of the political persecution of dissidents, and restoring of freedom of artistic and literary expression.[28] This was just too much for the Soviet Union to accept and for some of the satellites to witness. The hardliners felt that the movement was dangerous to the stability of communist regimes and had to be stopped.

On August 20 and 21, 1968, the Warsaw Pact countries led by the Soviet Union invaded Czechoslovakia. Dubcek was replaced in 1969 by a neo-Stalinist, Gustav Husak. The "Prague Spring" was turned into a "bitter cold winter." Canada and other Western countries expressed their sympathies for this East European country that had suffered humiliations three times in a period of thirty years, 1938, and 1948 and now in 1968. Inside Czechoslovakia a resistance group "Charter 77" was formed to counter the policies of the communist regime. Czechoslovakia continued to carry out her national and international commitments in a lackluster fashion until the demise of communism in 1989 in Eastern Europe. The people of the once great democratic state became despondent again according to reports sent to Ottawa by Canadian diplomats.

During the détente Czechoslovakia indicated a lukewarm attitude to the problem of family reunification.[29] The ministry of Interior had no sympathy for the dependents of defectors" or "escapees" who wished to be re-united with their husbands. Czechoslovakia did not accept the Helsinki Accords with enthusiasm. Grudgingly she agreed to a selective emigration. Canada was considered, by the Czech government, as an over-zealous defender of human rights frequently pointing her finger at the Soviet-bloc countries.

Canadian-Czechoslovak Hockey Games

International hockey competition today is common, but that was not the case in the early 1960s. At that time the Canadian government did not sponsor amateur sports and barely helped those competing in the Olympics. The athletes were on their own trying to scrape up enough money to pay for their traveling and accommodation expenses.

All competitions between countries evoked emotions but competitions between a Western and an Eastern- bloc country was particularly intense. Both sides maintained overtly or confidentially that their political system was superior to the other sides and therefore could produce better athletes. Because Eastern-bloc countries provided greater incentives for their athletes and used threats of punishment for poor athletic performances many athletes from Eastern Europe did exceptionally well.

A number of privately arranged exhibition junior games were held between Czechoslovakia and Canada in the early 1960s. It was soon discovered that there were many items that had to be attended to, namely, getting passports, visas, health certificates and proper authorization to travel to the Soviet-bloc countries. At best, adult travel to Eastern Europe was challenging. How much more challenging was it for teenagers?

One individual who tried to put hockey competition on a more or less semi-professional basis was Ken Dryden. He and his wife traveled to Czechoslovakia, investigated the quality of competition of that country and examined hockey-rink facilities.[30] He also had successful conversations with the Czechoslovak coaches and officials. The whole problem of eligibility was also discussed.

Altogether Dryden made four trips to Czechoslovakia ironing out difficulties that generally plague new beginnings. Not only were the Czechoslovaks satisfied with his effort, the Canadian government was also.[31] Some of the experiences gained were useful in arranging the Canada-USSR competition of the1970s.

Czechoslovak Commercial Relations

Czechoslovakia was one of Canada's best East European trading partners. During the years 1963-1968 Czechoslovak exports to Canada were second highest among the Soviet-bloc countries and her imports ranked fourth.[32] The main Canadian exports were wheat, nickel and asbestos. Canada tried to increase her trade by means of trade fairs and expositions had had trade counselors and promoters operating from Vienna.

As with Poland, Canada entered into pulpwood arrangements with Czechoslovakia. In 1978 H.A. Simons Limited of Vancouver signed a contract for building a pulp mill in Northern Slovakia at the cost of $300 million dollars.[33] This contract was expected to provide Canadians 10,000 man-years of employment.

Bilateral Relations with Other East European Countries

Pressured by Nazi Germany, Hungary, Romania and Bulgaria fought in World War II on the side of the Axis powers against the allies. Canada declared war on December 7, 1941, against Hungary and Romania but not on Bulgaria because the latter was a close friend of the Soviet Union who like Canada fought against Hitler. When the war was over the allies including Canada signed separate peace treaties[34] with the three East European countries dealing with such items as claims and war reparations.

Diplomatic relations with these countries were not established until the mid-1960s and early 1970s. In 1966 Bulgaria established diplomatic relations with Canada and reached an agreement with regards to claims and consular matters.[35] And on April 1967 Canada established diplomatic relations with Romania. In the same year Bulgaria opened an embassy in Ottawa. Bruce Williams, Canadian ambassador to Yugoslavia by dual accreditation became the first ambassador to Bulgaria and Romania.[36] At that period of time there was precious little outside trade with which the new ambassador had to deal.

Canadian-Hungarian Relations

Hungary was different. Since the Hungarian revolution there was a constant demand on British officials in Budapest to assist the Hungarian families who wished to contact their relatives in Canada. The British legation voiced a complaint that the demand on their time and energy was getting to the point of saturation. It was time for Canada to act. In 1967 a Canadian consul was posted in Budapest. Three years later Hungary opened an embassy in Ottawa but it wasn't until 1975 that Canada appointed T. Dilworth as an ambassador to Hungary and in 1976 J.E. Thibault became the first ambassador to Romania.[37]

Family reunification was one of the main issues during the détente that affected Canadian-Hungarian relation. During his tenure there was a significant increase of Canadians visiting Hungary and Hungarians visiting Canada. There was also a beginning of regular immigration to Canada.

Another item was trade. The secretary general of the Hungarian communist party, Janos Kadar, adopted a number of far-reaching reforms. One was to increase trade with other countries. He also introduced "New Economic Mechanism" which encouraged individual initiative and experimentation. And this "new class" of successful entrepreneurs made things happen. They paid less attention to ideology and more to empirical and experimental factors, which affected the country.

Other signs of developing relations between Canada and Hungary were evident in exchanges. Academic, scientific and cultural exchanges grew in leaps and bounds. Carleton University signed in 1974 an agreement with the Hungarian Institute of Culture Relations.[38] In the same year a Canada-Hungary Round table took place. In 1979 the Social Science, Humanities Research Council of Canada signed an important agreement with the Academy of Sciences of Hungary.[39]

Canadian-Romanian Bilateral Relations

Romanians were also active during the period of détente. Scientific, cultural, academic and economic exchanges also increased and high-level talks and parliamentary visit exchanges were frequent. These exchanges did not alter Canada's attitude towards human rights. She was critical of the human rights violations carried out by the rigid Nicolae Ceausescu regime but welcomed Romania's independent foreign policy.

The most important bilateral event in the1970s was the initiation of negotiations on the purchase of Canadian Candu reactors. Canada was willing to sell reactors to Romania provided that the latter agreed to abide by the terms of the non-Proliferation Treaty and to observe strictly the safeguards associated with these nuclear facilities. In 1977 the Atomic Energy of Canada Limited and Romanian and Canadian officials signed an agreement providing Romania with nuclear reactors. On her part, Romania agreed to maintain specific safeguards and to honour the terms of non-proliferation of nuclear power.[40]

Notes

[1] Memo from department of External Affairs (hereafter referred to as DEA) January 17, 1970, RG 25, volume 10839, National Archives of Canada (hereafter referred to as NAC).

[2] *Ibid.*

[3] Memorandum for the Minister, February 19, 1970, DEA *ibid.* files 20-1-3 Pol.vol 4.

[4] *Ibid.*

[5] *Ibid.*

[6] It was not entirely an open-door immigration policy for those who wished to immigrate to Canada had to satisfy Canada's occupational skills, health, needs, language, and security requirements.

[7] Memorandum for the Minister, September 23, 1971, RG 25 volume 10839 file 20-1-2, Pol v. 6, DEA.

[8] *Ibid.*

[9] *The Canadian Annual Review,* DEA, 1976.

[10] "Fisheries Relations," RG 25 volume 10839, file 20-1-2 Pol. DEA, Ottawa.

[11] *Ibid.*

[12] Under the agreement Canadian fishermen were permitted to fish on the Grand Banks and the Flemish Cap. See *Canadian Annual Review,* (hereafter cited as CAR) 1978.

[13] Canadian Polish Congress Meeting with Secretary of State for External Affairs, (hereafter cited as SSEA), February 1, 1971, RG 25 volume 10839, file 20-1-2, Pol DEA.

[14] *Ibid.*

[15] "Poland-Canadian Relations," *ibid.*

[16] *Ibid.*

[17] Although Tito withdrew from Cominform and the Warsaw Pact military organization he did not completely break his ties with Moscow.

[18] Memorandum to the Cabinet, November 8, 1950, RG 25 series 18 vol. 209, files Y-10-1, National Archives of Canada (hereafter cited as NAC).

[19] *The Canadian Annual Report,* 1951 Ottawa.

[20] SSEA to the Canadian embassy in Belgrade May 23, 1953, RG 25, file 10277-40, NAC.

[21] *Canadian Annual Review,* 1971, DEA, Ottawa.

[22] From the Metropolitan Toronto Police to Chief of Police, May 14, 1969, RG 25 file 22-8-2-21, pt. 3. DEA, NAC.

[23] Deputy Commissioner of Ontario Police, W.H. Kelley to DEA, November 1, 1968, *ibid.*

[24] From USSEA to the Canadian embassy in Belgrade, December 18, 1968, "Yugoslav National Day," DEA, *ibid.*

[25] "On Yugoslav Terrorism" October 8, 1969, *ibid.*

[26] From J.G.H Halstead, to Bruce Williams, Canadian Ambassador in Belgrade, November 28, 1969, *ibid.*

[27] From USSEA to the Canadian embassy in Prague, February 8, 1968 RG 25 volume 10502 file 55-73-mtl-G Czech 227.

[28] *Ibid.*

[29] *Ibid.*

[30] Memorandum on Hockey in Canada, December 2, 1974, RG 25 volume 10920, file 55-26-Hockey pt 2 DEA, NAC.

[31] *Ibid.*

[32] See Chapter VII.

[33] *Canadian Annual Review,* 1978, NAC.

[34] Canada, *Debates of the House of Commons,* 1947 pp. 229-230, volume I and 4819 volume V.

[35] *Canadian Annual Report,* 1967, DEA, Ottawa.

[36] *Ibid.*

[37] See *Canadian Annual Reports* 1967 and 1976, DEA, Ottawa.

[38] *Canadian Annual Report,* 1974, DEA.

[39] *Ibid.* 1979, DEA.

[40] *Ibid.* 1974, DEA.

VII. CANADA'S TRADE WITH EASTERN EUROPE

As one of the world's greatest trading nations, Canada eagerly sought markets for her raw materials and manufactured goods. While maintaining the traditional role of supplying grain and industrial raw materials to Eastern Europe, Canada attempted to diversify and increase her exports of semi- and fully-manufactured goods. One of the main reasons for Canada opening legations in Eastern Europe was to initiate and maintain trade with foreign countries.

Taking the year 1975 we note that the value of imports from Eastern Europe was about $159 million dollars. The import-export Canadian trade with foreign countries depended on demand and supply principles. If Canadians required certain goods some of which were produced or manufactured in Eastern Europe, then companies or enterprises would try to meet these requests. Among the Canadian imports in 1975 were, fabrics, textile products, footwear, bicycles, foodstuffs, wines and specialized machinery.[1] In return Canada continued to sell to Eastern Europe technology and grain.

Canada had trade agreements with all East European countries on Tariffs and Trade (GATT) basis.[2] Bilateral agreements with these countries provided provisions for consultations allowing Canada to identify import and export priorities. Although Canada did not have an agreement equal to INDEXAG (Agreement on Co-operation in the Industrial Application of Science and Technology) made with the Soviet Union in 1971), she did have trade and technology contacts with Poland, Rumania, Hungary, Bulgaria and Czechoslovakia from time to time. There was another important reason for Canada to develop trade with Eastern Europe. Following the signing of the Helsinki Accords in 1975 Canada took upon herself to promote détente by "building mutual trust and confidence" between East and West. One way of doing this was through negotiations associated with commercial contracts.

During the post-Helsinki period trade consultants, experts in agriculture, urban development, energy, fisheries, air travel and nuclear co-operation—visits that were reciprocated by Canadian counterparts, inundated Canada.

Table I: **Canadian Exports** ($000)

Country	**1963-1969**	**1970-1979**	**1980-1986**
Bulgaria	43,049	3,423	126,369
Czechoslovakia	141,367	135,913	259,587
Hungary	39,532	68,511	104,779
Poland	224,367	1,073,685	1,189,728
Romania	9,425	225,799	238,052
Yugoslavia	80,162	319,329	449,051

Dominion Bureau of Statistics, Canada Year Book, 1963-1986

Table II: **Canadian Imports** ($000)

Country	**1963-1969**	**1970-1979**	**1980-1986**
Bulgaria	6,801	27,551	45,373
Czechoslovakia	173,158	155,167	445,724
Hungary	39,095	153,213	216,825
Poland	94,410	398,290	412,969
Romania	16,128	197,501	313,344
Yugoslavia	31,418	147,189	244,293

Dominion Bureau of Statistics, Canada Year Book, 1963-1986

As Tables I and II indicate, Poland was Canada's best customer in import-export trade. Although Canada exported raw materials and manufactured goods to Poland, the chief export was grain. (See Table III). Czechoslovakia ranked the second largest importer of Canadian products and Yugoslavia the second largest exporter of goods to Canada. Romania remained the third best overall import-export East European country with whom Canada traded.

Commercial and trade exchanges were not the only means used to increase trade. Trade fairs and exhibitions became common. Canada participated in important fairs in 1969 at Poznan, Poland; Zagreb, Yugoslavia and Brno, Czechoslovakia.[3] Again in 1982 and 1983 Canada again took part in fairs that provided East Europeans a view of Canadian products produced and available for sale.

The Helsinki Accords notwithstanding, Canada did not enjoy unrestricted avenue to trade with the Soviet Union and Eastern Europe. At the time of crises created by the Soviet Union or her satellites, NATO imposed sanctions on goods going to the country or goods produced by the satellites. For instance, the Soviet Union's invasion of Afghanistan and the imposition of martial law by the Polish government led to NATO's sanctions on the Soviet Union.

Although Canada was anxious to develop trade with Eastern Europe she was not ready to do so if it violated some of the cardinal principles of Canada's foreign policy. One such case occurred when Hungary wanted to conclude a commercial treaty with Canada in 1956. The departments of External Affairs and Trade were opposed to the suggested treaty for a number of reasons. First of all, they argued that such a treaty would not increase trade significantly and secondly, the proliferation of East European posts or trade missions would only create new security problems. The head of the Economic Division of the department of External Affairs argued that the establishment of a Hungarian trade mission would "open new opportunities for Hungarian espionage in Canada and impose a further strain on the already over taxed resources of our security services." [4]

There were two other arguments used against the negotiation of a commercial treaty.[5] According to a senior member in the department of External Affairs, such a treaty would not lessen the tensions between East and West, but on the contrary, might probably increase them.[6] Finally, the signing of the treaty with a country that was persecuting Cardinal Jozsef Mindszenty would displease Roman Catholics and some ethnic Canadians.

Other Factors in the East-West Trade

A large percentage of Canada's export trade with Eastern Europe was in grain. Of all the East European countries in this study Poland was the most consistent buyer of Canadian wheat. (See Table III). Poland did grow wheat and other cereals but it was insufficient for her population. The old-fashioned methods of cultivation of land by horses or small tractors could not produce enough food for the growing urban population. In addition, the communist regime was reluctant to provide the farmers with chemical fertilizers to improve the fertility of the soil. The soil in Poland was not as productive as the soil in Hungary, Bulgaria or Romania. Whereas such countries as Czechoslovakia and East Germany were using farming practices, comparable to that found in Western Europe to improve their grain yields Poland was not.

Table III: **Canadian Wheat Exports to Eastern Europe, 1968-1975**

(1000 tonnes)

Country	**Year 1969**	**Year 1970**	**Year 1971**	**Year 1972**	**Year 1973**	**Year 1974**	**Year 1975**	**Total**
Bulgaria		52						52
Czechoslovakia				16				16
Hungary	80							80
Poland	93	103	50	77	74	108	64	569

Source: *Statistics Canada, Grain Trade of Canada*

Besides the changes in agriculture, there were noticeable attempts made by East European countries to improve industrial production and to change from command economy to a free market economy. In Hungary Kadar introduced in 1968 a program called the New Economic Mechanism[7] and Yugoslavia experimented with Workers' Self-Management, both of which incorporated decentralization of industries and enterprises and stressed individual initiative. To some extent Poland departed from the traditional, Soviet-type central planning in the late 1960s. In 1967 Czechoslovakia introduced innovative economic and political reforms only to have them suppressed in 1968 by the Soviet Union and some of her satellites.

As Table IV shows that over 65 percent of East European trade was with socialist countries. In order to carry out their economic reforms these socialist countries had to buy from trade Western countries the much- needed technology and manufactured goods. Romania was the first East European country to lessen her dependency on CMEA markets, a trend that was followed by Poland in the early 70s. Bulgaria, as expected, adhered to the

CMEA (Council for Mutual Economic Assistance). Yugoslavia, who opted out from the socialist family in 1949, carried on a brisk trade with the West.

Table IV: **Share of Trade with CMEA Countries as percent of Total Trade**

(Percentages)

Country	1960	1965	1970	1971	1972	1973	1974
Bulgaria							
Import	80.3	70.3	73.0	74.4	78.1	77.1	68.0
Export	80.7	75.8	75.8	75.8	78.2	77.4	72.9
Czechoslovakia							
Import	64.6	64.5	62.3	63.1	63.9	61.3	54.9
Export	61.4	66.2	61.8	64.9	66.0	64.6	63.4
Poland							
Import	58.1	61.7	65.8	64.2	58.2	49.4	42.3
Export	55.0	59.3	60.5	59.4	60.6	58.2	53.0
Romania							
Import	67.9	57.5	48.3	46.3	45.4	40.7	32.9
Export	65.8	63.7	50.3	48.0	47.8	45.5	36.5

Source: *The Economic Development of the CMEA Countries, 1950-1968*, Warsaw and *The CMEA Countries: Population, Economy, Culture*, Warsaw. 1972

Détente and particularly the Helsinki Accords opened the doors for a change in Eastern European commerce. Eastern Europeans were hungry for Western technologies and the Western way of life. To achieve this the governments began to borrow money in order to purchase machinery and technology from the West. At the same time communist-satellite countries began to increase their trade with the Western world. Ordinarily, the bulk of the trade in the East European bloc was with communist countries with the exception of Yugoslavia who traded with the West and with the CMEA at the same time. In order to obtain Western currencies to buy Western technology they needed to borrow money.

Table V: **East European Net Currency Debt, 1970-1977**

($billons)

Country	1970	1974	1975	1976	1977
Bulgaria	.7	1.2	1.8	2.3	2.7
Czechoslovakia	.3	1.1	1.5	2.1	2.7
Hungary	.6	1.5	2.1	2.8	3.4
Poland	.8	3.9	6.9	10.2	13.0
Romania	1.2	2.6	3.0	3.3	4.0
Yugoslavia	7.9	5.4	6.6	7.9	9.9

Source: This statistical data was compiled by Paul Marer and contained in his article entitled, "East European Economies: Achievements, Problems, Prospects" and published in *Communism In Eastern Europe*, edited by Teresa Rakowska-Harmstone and Andrew Gyorgy, Indiana University Press.

But borrowing increased the total debt of the six East European countries from $5 billion in 1970 to $32 billion by the end of 1977. Ideally the borrowed money was to help modernize the industries whose products could then be sold abroad to recoup the investments. That did not materialize due to the soaring world energy commodity prices and economic recession in the West. Table V shows the Soviet and East European debt from 1970 to 1977. Poland led East European countries in this area as she and other Soviet bloc countries took the advantage of détente to borrow money hoping that the money invested in industries and enterprises would enable them to repay the loans. There was plenty of cash floating around generated by OPEC countries and deposited in Western banks for Eastern European countries' consumption.

Patterns of Negotiations with East European States

East European countries favoured long-term contracts whereas Western countries leaned towards shorter agreements, which could benefit free market economies. The communist five or seven-year plans were not affected by world prices which were based on the principles of supply and demand. They were fixed for the duration of the plan.

One of the first countries to negotiate a short-term contract was Yugoslavia when Canada sold her wheat under section 21 of the Export Insurance Act in the years 1952, 1954, 1963 and 1971.[8] The last sale amounted to ten million dollars. Poland bought wheat and barley on a short-term contract from the years 1956 to 1962 and on long-term contracts from 1963 to 1989. Rollimpex was the Polish agency with which the Canada Wheat Board negotiated. Canada also negotiated wheat deals with Czechoslovakia in the late 50s and mid 60s. Because Czechoslovakia had a more balanced trade she was able to pay for the wheat partly or wholly through her exports.

Most of other East European countries that purchased wheat or barley received from Canada loans under the Export Credit Insurance Act. Two countries in particular, Poland and Yugoslavia, availed themselves of this arrangement.[9] Unlike Czechoslovakia these two countries' imports far exceeded their exports to Canada.

Entrance of three other East European Countries

In the 1960s the other three East European states, Hungary, Bulgaria and Romania expressed their desire to enjoy the same Most Favoured Nation (MFN) status as Poland, Czechoslovakia and Yugoslavia had. Bulgaria agreed to buy 100,000 tons of Canadian wheat and flour each year for three years and pay ten percent on a credit loan equal to twenty-four million dollars.[10] The same agreement gave Bulgaria an access for her ships to Canadian ports and the right to open a trade office in Canada. Bulgarian negotiators hoped to investigate the possibility of selling some Bulgarian products.

When it came to Hungary, Canada had sentimental feelings towards a country that less than eight years before had suffered much at the hands of the Soviet Union. There was no longer the problem of barring her because she belonged to the communist bloc. At the same time Canada required that, as in the case of Bulgaria, that Hungary make a commitment to buy a specified quantity of wheat, flour and barley.[11]

Canada's negotiations with Romania were long and rather difficult. Back in 1963 the Cabinet authorized the government to explore the possibility of a trade agreement similar to the one Canada negotiated with Hungary and Bulgaria. Romania was anxious to sell Canada corn, timber and petroleum, products that Canada had in abundance. But Canada produced some of the products that Romania wanted to sell, particularly grain and nickel. However, Canada was eager to purchase petrol-chemical products from Romania. As with other East European countries Ottawa's negotiations for a trade treaty was dependent upon Romania's purchase of grain, an exchange of diplomats and a satisfactory settlement of claims. After extensive negotiations Romania agreed to buy $15 million dollars worth of Canadian products chiefly wheat, pay a lump sum of money as a settlement of claims and was ready to exchange diplomats.[12] In July 1972 the bilateral agreement was signed.

Notes

---

[1] C.L. Bland, "Trading with Eastern Europe," *Canada Commerce*, June-July, 1976, p. 2.

[2] *Ibid.* p. 4.

[3] *Canadian Annual Report*, 1968.

[4] R.A.D. Ford to the minister of Trade, May 11, 1956, RG 25, volume 6248, and file 9376-A-40 pt. 1, National Archives of Canada, hereafter noted as NAC.

[5] *Ibid.*

[6] L.B. Pearson's memorandum on the trade Agreement with Hungary, May 22, 1956, *ibid.*

[7] Bennett Kovrig, "Hungary", *Communism in Eastern Europe*, edited by Teresa Rakowska-Harmstone and Andrew Gyorgy, Indiana University Press, pp. 88-90 and "Yugoslavia" by Robin Alison Remington, pp. 218-219.

[8] Memorandum to the Cabinet, May 1972, department of Trade and Commerce, volume 223, file 20-141-y1, NAC, Ottawa.

[9] Proposed agreement with regards to the sale of wheat, April 13, 1967, P.C.1967-695, RG 20 department of Trade and Commerce, volume 2327, NAC.

[10] Memorandum to the Cabinet, May 31, 1966, department of Trade and Commerce, box 5194, file 8810/B933-2-pt 2, NAC.

[11] Memorandum to the Cabinet, December 22, 1964, RG 20, volume 2637, file 20E-2R-2-1, NAC.

[12] *Ibid.*

VIII. POPE JOHN PAUL II AND THE DEMISE OF COMMUNISM

Canada and the newly elected Pope John Paul II had similar goals for Eastern Europe. Freedom of speech, religion, movement and assembly were deep and fundamental aspirations of Canadians and of Pope John Paul. Over and over again the Pope and the Canadian government defended the inalienable rights of human beings, regardless of colour, class or religion. Generally speaking the Canadian Charter of Rights and Freedoms reflected many of the Pope's ideas on freedom found in his encyclicals and his instructions to the Catholics.

Many years before the ascent of Pope John Paul II the Canadian government had expressed concern about religious persecution in Eastern Europe. In the early years of the Cold War the Canadian minister of External Affairs, L.B. Pearson[1] broached the topic of religious persecution in the House of Commons noting that Catholic priests, Lutheran and Calvinist ministers were targets of communist persecutions[2] Prominent Catholic prelates suffered humiliating treatment at the hands of the communists, among them being Cardinal Joszef Mindszenty of Hungary, the Croatian Cardinal Alojzije Stepaniac, the Czech bishop Josef Beran, the Ukrainian metropolitan, Josyj Slipyj and the Polish primate, Cardinal Stefan Wyszynski.

Canada was not satisfied to voice her concerns about religious persecution in the House of Commons; she also participated in a universal condemnation of the countries that were responsible for such persecution. As a signatory of the Paris Peace Treaties of March 30, 1947, with Bulgaria, Hungary and Rumania, Canada, through the office of the United States and in consort with the governments of the United Kingdom and the United States, drew up a resolution condemning human rights violations. In addition to the condemnation of the violation of the Treaties, Canada dispatched R.M Macdonell, the charge d'affaires stationed in Prague, to ascertain the scope of the violations.[3] Macdonnel found the attitude of the communist regime hypocritical and unacceptable.

The condemnation of the violation of the Treaties did not terminate the persecution of Christians in Eastern Europe. Time and again Catholic priests, sisters and brothers were imprisoned, Church properties confiscated and nationalized the teaching of religion in schools prohibited and church services interfered with. Communist regimes permitted and even encouraged divorces and abortions that were forbidden by most Christian churches.

During the Cold War period the persecution intensified. Cardinal Wyszynski was put under house arrest (1950-1953) and Cardinal Mindszenty sought refuge in the American embassy (1956), for the communist authorities sought to arrest and try him on allegations of treason. Whereas the Catholic Church in Hungary and Czechoslovakia succumbed to the intense pressure from the communist regimes, the Catholic Church in Poland under the leadership of Cardinal Wyszynski continued to challenge the communist regime by insisting that the Polish people had an inherent right to practice their religion. He did not hesitate to condemn abortion and the use of public tax money to spread atheism.[4]

The Church's policy of dealing with the communists varied from one pope to another. Popes Pius XI and Pius XII considered communism an evil that needed to be combated vigorously. In his encyclical, *Divini Redemptoris*, Pius XI labeled the communist doctrine as "a false messianic idea" in which a "pseudo-ideal of justice" is portrayed. He called for a Church campaign against world communism under the patronage of St. Joseph, the patron of workers. His successor, Pope Pius XII, (1939-1958) went further when he called on all Christians to participate in a crusade against the communist peril.

The next three popes adopted a more conciliatory policy towards the communists. Pope John XXIII (1958-1963) was open to dialogue with the communists hoping that his new approach would result in ushering "a socialism with a human face." He firmly believed that the policy of "confrontation" would only lead to increased tensions. The summoning of a Council to which Catholics of different views were invited demonstrated his "openness" to new ideas. He himself set the example by the manner he conducted the deliberations at the Vatican II Council. His approach was continued by his successors, Pope Paul VI (1963-1978) and Pope John Paul II (1978-) In the spirit of the Helsinki Accords and the Conference on Security and Cooperation in Europe the Vatican diplomats in the service of Pope Paul VI had cordial conversations with the Soviet and East European diplomats. Instead of shying away from the communists, Paul VI warmly welcomed them at the Vatican. His "one step at a time" concept and his support for the human rights provisions of "basket" three of the Helsinki Accords helped to open the doors for the eventual freeing of Eastern Europe from communist regimes.

Pope John Paul II Ready to Meet Challenges

The dialogue of Popes John XXIII and Paul VI with the communists prepared the road for further contacts between the East and the West and between the Catholic Church and the rest of the world. No other Pope had such personal contacts with the communists as John Paul. As a Pole who experienced repression under the Nazis and later the communists, Pope John Paul demonstrated insights and courage. He was not afraid of the communists; he knew their tactics and their ideology well enough to refute their falsehood but at the same time he invited them to a dialogue. As a member of the Slavic family he fully appreciated the customs and traditions of all East Europeans. At the same time his mind was open to western ideas be they social, literary, philosophical or theological. With two doctorates, one in theology and the other in philosophy, he was academically ready for a senior post in the Catholic Church. His gift of leadership did not escape the notice of his superiors. In 1957 Pope Pius XII named him bishop of Cracow and in 1967 he received the cardinal's hat from Pope Paul VI. He took an active role in the Vatican II Council where he delivered two very important position papers, one on liturgical reforms and the other on the Church as a people of God. In addition, he addressed the Council on topics related to lay responsibility, religious freedom and the Church in the modern world. His contributions to the Council made Cardinal Karol Wojtyla one of the best-known and respected cardinals in the Consistory. It was not a great surprise that he was short-listed for the highest position in the Catholic Church and elected pope on October 16, 1978.[5]

Immediate Reaction to the Polish Pope

As expected, Poles, in Poland and those in the diaspora were happy to learn about the result of the election. Some Canadians of Polish extraction had met him when in 1967 as Cardinal Wojtyla, he had visited a number of Polish communities in Canada on his way back to Poland after attending a Eucharistic Congress in the United States. The Canadian-Polish Congress, on behalf of all Canadian Poles, warmly welcomed the newly elected pope.

Whereas the Western press wrote favourably of the new pope, the Soviet Union showed signs of nervousness and consternation. Following the day of the election, the head of the KGB, Yuri Andropov, phoned the KGB agent in Warsaw chastising him for allowing a member of the satellite country to become a pope. In his opinion, the pope could disturb the "stability of communism in Poland and throughout the world." Above all the Kremlin feared that the new Polish pope would demand more religious freedom for the people of Eastern Europe. A respected Kremlinologist, Oleg Bogomolov, mused that the nationalists in Lithuania, Belorussia and Ukraine would agitate more vigorously for independence and the Greek Catholics in Western Ukraine would stir up trouble. Little did the Soviet officials realize that the new pope would not be paralyzed by the reaction of communist leaders. With strong convictions and a clear notion of his mission he agreed to address the United Nations.

A Defender of Human Rights

Greeted by the secretary general of the United Nations, Kurt Waldheim, Pope John Paul walked into the secretarial building projecting vigor, energy and quiet strength. As an amateur actor he knew how to charm the audience through his smiles and friendly gestures. He did not waste time to deal with one of his favorite topics, human rights. Referring to the United Nations Universal Declaration of Human Rights he stated that peace could only be attained if the inalienable rights of individuals and communities were respected." He then went on to spell out what the rights were: "the right to freedom of thought, conscience…and the right to manifest one's religion either individually or in community, in public or in private." [7]

The topic of religious freedom was nothing new for the Pope, for it was fully discussed at the end of the fourth session of the Vatican Council who issued the Declaration on Religious Freedom. The Bishops from Central and Eastern Europe had warmly endorsed the Declaration even in the face of the continued persecution by communist regimes. In its adoption of the Declaration, the Council stated that the right to religious freedom had its foundation in the very dignity of the human person, and that this dignity was known through the revealed Word of God and reason. In addition, the right of each human person to exercise religious freedom was universally recognized in constitutional law as a civil right.[8]

The Pope in 1980 reiterated the 1965 Vatican Council statement in his address to UNESCO. In September of the same year he sent personal letters to the heads of the thirty-five countries who had signed the Helsinki Agreement urging them to conscientiously review the records of human rights violations and report these violations at the Madrid Conference. Canada, one of the signatories of the Agreement, along with Denmark, was selected to observe violations of human rights, particularly in those areas pertaining to the three of Baskets of the Helsinki Accords.

Pope John Paul II defended the basic rights of all men and women and not just the institutional rights of the Catholic Church. Fully cognizant of the rights of each government he argued that these rights must not denigrate the basic human rights. He rejected the concept of the human person held by communists who claimed that every man and woman was the property of the state. According to Pope John Paul the very nature of a human being sets him or her free from state's unreasonable restrictions.

The Pope's First Visit to Poland

After his election Pope John Paul was most anxious to visit his homeland. He loved the Polish people and wanted to help them spiritually, diplomatically and psychologically. He fully realized how much they suffered under a communist regime. As the head of the largest Christian religion in the world and a recognized spiritual world leader he longed to give his people hope and confidence in themselves. Fully aware of the Polish government's refusal to permit his predecessor, Pope Paul VI, to attend the millennium celebration in 1966, Pope John Paul II attempted to convince the Polish government of the importance for the head of the Catholic Church to attend the 900th-year anniversary of the martyrdom of Saint Stanislaw, the first bishop of Cracow. It was one thing to have a strong anti-communist head of the Catholic Church in Rome, but it was something else to have him on the Polish soil and among the Polish people.

Pope John Paul's popularity and his high position did not eliminate the opposition to such a visit from the Soviet authorities. One of the leading opponents to his visit was Leonid Brezhnev, the communist party leader of the Soviet Union. He directed Edward Gierek, the secretary of the Polish United Workers' Party, to drum up excuses for refusing the Pope's request to visit Poland, arguing that such a visit would cause undue problems for Poland and for Eastern Europe. The Polish leader refused to follow the urgings of Brezhnev and instead welcomed the Pope.

On June 2, 1979 Pope John Paul arrived at the Warsaw airport greeted by the Polish president, Henryk Jablonski and the primate, Cardinal Wyszynski amidst the jubilant tolling of church bells. Although this was his first visit to his native land as a Pope, it was a also a pilgrimage for him to many historic and sacred places like Gniezno, the city whose ancient church contained the relics of St. Adalbert, the first missionary to Poland; to the shrine of the black Madonna at Czestochowa; to the beautiful city of Cracow where Pope John was consecrated bishop and to Auschwitz, the scene of many atrocities committed by the Nazis. Everywhere the Pope went thousands and thousands of people gathered to see and hear him. But it was in his favourite city of Cracow where he called the Polish people to continue to have faith, love, courage and hope.

> You must be strong with the strength of faith, he said...You must be strong with the strength of hope that brings the perfect joy of life and does not allow us to grieve the Holy Spirit. You must be strong with love, which is stronger than death...and helps us to set up a great dialogue with man and the world rooted in the dialogue with God Himself, with the Father through the Son in the Holy Spirit, the dialogue of salvation.[9]

The nine-day pilgrimage inspired the Poles with a sense of self-worth and optimism. The Polish people were convinced that the Pope would not let them down but instead support them in their struggle to become free and independent. They knew that the Pope rejected the decisions of the Yalta and Potsdam conferences. He encouraged his people to have patience and hope, sentiments that all Eastern European satellites were glad to hear.

Pope John Paul's Principles Are Tested

Pope John Paul firmly believed that communism could be eliminated in Eastern Europe not by military force but by peaceful means. He argued that communism could be countered by non-violence, truth, solidarity and responsibility.[10] To live "in the truth" he said is to reject the culture of "lies" and "pretence". Each person, he said, is asked to take his/hers responsibility of "living in the truth" seriously, not only with himself/herself but with others.

Nowhere were the principles espoused by Pope John Paul more severely tested than in Poland. Coming from a country that was partitioned in the 18th century by Russia, Austria and Prussia, and again in the 20th century by the Soviet Union and Nazi Germany and later made a satellite by Moscow, Pope John Paul understood the ramifications of resistance. The spirit of freedom and independence was deeply imbedded in the hearts and souls of each Pole. During the 19th and the 20th centuries Poles rose up against their oppressors and conquerors. In 1830-31, 1846-48 and the 1863 rebellions the Poles fought the Russian Czars whereas in 1956, 1970, and 1976 and in 1980-1981 they battled against the communist overlords. The spirit of nationalism coupled with their Catholic faith gave Poles the courage, strength and even the enthusiasm to resist the "enemies" against all odds. The slogan "Poland is not lost while we are alive" sums up the survival instinct of the Polish nation.

East European communist satellites were not content with their Soviet overlords. East Germany and Poland rebelled against the political and economic constraints in 1953, Hungary in 1956 and Czechoslovakia in 1968.[11] Tito challenged the Soviet power in 1949 by refusing to have Yugoslavia follow the dictates of Stalin. But it was in Poland where the resistance was consistent and pervasive resulting in the formation of a ten-million strong association, Solidarity. Led by an unemployed electrician, Lech Walesa, Solidarity forced the resignation of the communist leader, Edward Gierek, who was unable to bring a solution to the economic problems facing the nation. The underlying irritant was not only economic, but political as well. The Poles vehemently resented the Soviet imposed regime. Instead of cultivating a meaningful dialogue with the Polish people under the new leader, General Wojciech Jaruzelski, encouraged by the Kremlin authorities, declared martial law in Poland on December 13, 1981. A year before the imposition of martial law Pope John Paul, alarmed by the growing discontent of the people and by the threat of an invasion by the Soviet Union, wrote a letter to Leonid Brezhnev calling on him to help defuse the existing tensions. He referred to the Soviet Union's solemn commitment to the principles of the Helsinki Final Act which each of the signatories, including the Soviet Union, had promised to respect particularly the principle of non-intervention in the affairs of each participating country.[12]

One does not know the effect this letter had on the Soviet decision to refrain from invading Poland, a decision that was made in the first week of December 1980. There were a number of reasons for this decision. Intelligence sources indicated that the Polish people and even some of the army units would have resisted a Soviet-led force. In addition, the premier of Poland, General Jaruzelski, convinced the Kremlin that Poland was able to solve her own problems without outside assistance. The Pope also insisted that the Poles have the undeniable rights to solve their problems themselves. At the same time he urged the Polish government to use dialogue rather than confrontation. He supported the right of the workers to form their union,[13] a right that he termed as inalienable and natural.

The Pope decided to get involved in the solution of the explosive problem by going to Poland during the crisis. Ostensibly he wanted to participate in the celebration of the anniversary of the Black Madonna of Jasna Gora, but in reality he came to Poland to give his people courage to face the crisis. He arrived in Warsaw on June 16, 1983 in circumstances very different from those in 1979 soon after he was elected Pope. Poland was now under martial law, Solidarity was dissolved and its leaders imprisoned. He felt that he was standing "beneath the cross of Christ with all his country men and women whose freedom was taken away and (whose) dignity was trampled."[14] Everywhere he visited he cautioned the people to be patient, have faith in the Mother of Jasna Gora and be hopeful. He showed that he possessed a strong abiding hope himself when he agreed to see the head of the state, General Jaruzelski and reminded him that the "social renewal" about which the communists constantly spoke of would not occur unless the fundamental rights of mankind were recognized. Several months after meeting the Polish premier martial law was lifted and many of the Solidarity members were set free.

The Pope's visit to Poland at the time of the imposition of martial law was significant in other ways. Very adroitly the Pope was able to pressure General Jaruzelski to dialogue with the Church and the workers without enhancing the Government's authority or provoking violence. Quoting the late Cardinal Wyszynski he stressed that it was the people's inherent right to organize unions and the state's duty was to protect these rights.[15] Walesa's meeting with the Pope on his last day of visit indicated his position regarding unions. The Polish people were convinced that the Pope would continue to support the cause of freedom and independence even from outside of Poland. They were not alone, for other people of Eastern Europe felt the same way being convinced that they had in Rome a staunch defender of human rights.

The Canadian Connection

What was happening in Poland was of concern to Canada. Although Canada was not involved in the decisions drawing-up of the Potsdam and Yalta Conferences, she nevertheless followed the roller coaster pattern of the Polish state under Nazi Germany and later on under the heel of the Soviet Union. Canadians of all national and religious stripes sympathized with the gallant Poles as they struggled to be free and independent. Canadians of Polish origin, whether born in Canada or naturalized Canadians, demonstrated special interest for the affairs of Poland. On a number of occasions the Canadian-Polish Congress, which represented Canadian-Polish interests made interventions on behalf of Polish immigrants, sending food and medical supplies to needy people of Poland and defended the legitimate rights of the Polish Canadians. Pope John Paul's influence was recognized, his leadership uncontested and his worldwide Christian message telecast throughout the world. Whether one agreed with the Pope's teaching or not, one was struck by his charisma. Whereas many politicians followed the course of "political correctness" Pope John Paul spoke openly on many sensitive moral issues. And for this he was admired.

Canada understood the importance of Pope's leadership in the quest for peace and freedom. The Canadian government was informed by the Canadian embassy in Warsaw what was transpiring in Poland during the rise of the Solidarity movement. In a confidential memo "Communist Policy and Tactics – Pope's Visit to Poland" the Canadian Department of External Affairs detailed the events of his 1983 visit to Poland. The Canadian government was concerned that the Pope's visit during the critical period of the imposition of martial law might engender riots and demonstrations. The Canadian official who personally followed the Pope's visit was impressed with the peace and order that prevailed during his visit....

Despite the peaceful visit of the Pope, Canada and her NATO partners did not rush to lift the imposed sanctions on Poland. They followed the policy of "wait and see" whether the Polish government was willing to respect the legitimate demands of the workers, the Church and the common people. The Canadian-Polish Congress urged the Polish government to lift martial law, release the detained Solidarity leaders and open negotiations. The Canadian government also agreed in principle with the demands of the Congress but Prime Minister Pierre Trudeau expressed his own opinion on the events in Poland. He considered Solidarity just another labour union, which was constantly demanding higher wages. Instead of commending the Solidarity for its heroic defence of human rights, among which was the right to form a democratic labour union he chastised it for causing a situation which might have offended the Soviet Union and affected the détente. The remarks of Trudeau infuriated many Canadians particularly Canadians of Polish orign. The secretary of state for External Affairs, Mark McGuigan attempted to defuse the issue by adopting a position that was more favourable to the ethnic groups.

The Polish ambassador to Canada called on McGuigan on December 3, 1982 to discuss a variety of issues affecting Canadian-Polish relations. During the course of the conversation, such topics of mutual interest as trade, arms race, lifting of martial law, and deferment of Polish debts, release of internees, and the deployment of missiles in Western Europe were discussed. To the ambassador's question as to when Canada would lift her sanctions against Poland, the undersecretary said that it would depend on a number of factors, one of which was the results of the Pope's visit to Poland.[16]

In 1983 martial law was lifted but the NATO sanctions continued to be imposed because the Polish government was not willing to eliminate restrictions similar to those of martial law. Although Solidarity was not restored there were signs of significant changes in Poland. The new Soviet leader, Mikhail Gorbachev, who took power in 1985, made it possible for changes in Eastern Europe to take place. He assured the Eastern bloc countries that the Soviet Union would not interfere with their quest for independence. He thought that a "controlled liberalization" could take place without dismantling the Soviet Union. His hopes were dashed as Poland, Hungary, Czechoslovakia, East Germany and Bulgaria shed their communist regimes, became independent and elected their own parliaments. Gorbachev with his two-prong policies, "glasnost" and "perestroika" tried to give an example of how the new freedoms and structures could operate within a communist state but failed to win over the Soviet people.

Who was responsible for the demise of the Soviet Empire?

Historians and political scientists have probed deeply to find the answer to this question. They discovered that there was no single answer as a number of events and individuals factored into the equation. Eastern Europe was opened to change instigated by the Conference on Security and Co-operation in Europe and by its product, the Helsinki Accords. The on-going review conferences in Belgrade, Madrid and Vienna monitored violations of human rights creating avenues of freedom.

Three individuals stand out who encouraged, led or assisted in the demise of the Soviet Empire. Mikhail Gorbachev was one of them.[17] By assuring Eastern bloc countries that they were free to decide their destiny, be it communist or democratic, he lifted one of the great impediments to freedom and independence. The Brezhnev doctrine was dead. Gorbachev was a practical communist who tried ways and means of improving the Soviet Union's economic and political structures. His interest in a free Eastern Europe was similar to that of Pope John Paul.

Another leader, President Ronald Reagan, also had conversations with the Pope on matters of peace and security. The American president had little use for the Soviet Union calling it "an evil empire." Governed by fear and distrust of the Soviet Union he initiated a continental defence called "the Star Wars." Although this project did not see the light of day, it did create in the Soviet Union an atmosphere of panic. Brezhnev and his successors spent millions of dollars on defence to the detriment of consumer goods and the quality of life for the Soviet people. In an attempt to keep up with the United States the Soviet rulers left their country prostrated and virtually bankrupt. These conditions made Gorbachev welcome.

The last of the individuals who had an outstanding influence on the demise of the Soviet Union was Pope John Paul II. He was not only a moral and spiritual leader but also a world leader. Presidents, prime ministers, religious leaders and royalties took the advantage of having a papal audience with him. At the time of political, social, economic and religious upheavals, the Pope stood "tall," championing the poor, the marginalized and the dispossessed. Everywhere he went he defended the inalienable rights of all people irrespective of religion, colour, political affiliation or nationality. On a number of occasions he came to the defense of Christians in Eastern Europe. He not only welcomed visitors at the Vatican, he traveled to meet them in their own country. In a way he was a citizen of the world.

Knowing what type of a man the Pope was, what he said and did, would Eastern Europe have become free and independent without his presence? Would Poland have been able to resist the Soviet regime without the help of the Pope? Would there have been a peaceful, non-violent transformation in Eastern Europe without his influence? The answers to these questions will throw light on the influence of this man.

Notes

[1] Memorandum on Religious Persecution in Eastern Europe, March 16, 1950, Department of External Affairs, (hereafter noted as DEA) National Archives of Canada, (hereafter noted as NAC).

[2] Statement made by L.B. Pearson in the house of Commons, February 2, 1949, *Canada, debates of the House of Commons*, Ottawa.

[3] Final report of an ad hoc Political Committee, May 2, 1950, Department of External Affairs (hereafter noted as DEA files.) NAC, Ottawa.

[4] Aloysius Balawyder, *In the Clutches of the Kremlin, Canadian-East European Relations,* East European Monographs, 2000, p.108.

[5] For an exhaustive account of the life and the achievements of Pope John Paul II see George Weigel's biography of the Pope, *Witness to Hope*, Cliff Street Books, 1999.

[6] *Ibid.*

[7] Pope John Paul's address to the 34th Assembly of the United Nations, United Nations publication, p .5.

[8] Quoted in George Weigel's book *Witness to Hope*, p.165.

[9] *Ibid.* p.319-320.

[10] George Weigel, *The Final Revolution: The Resistant Church and the Collapse of Communism*, Oxford University Press, 1992, p.52.

[11] Adam Bromke, "Poland and Hungary in 1956," found in *Poland, The Last Decade*, Mosaic Press, 1981, pp.112-116 and pp. 148-163.

[12] A letter send to Leonid Brezhnev by Pope Jon Paul II on December 16, 1980, quoted in *Witness to Hope*, 406-407.

[13] *Ibid.* 463

[14] *Ibid.* p.461.

[15] " Pope's Visit to Poland" a confidential dispatch from the Canadian Embassy in Warsaw to Department of External Affairs, June 28, 1983, DEA files, 20-Poland-1-16-8.

[16] Discussion between ambassador Pawlak and the under-secretary, December 3, 1982, department of External Affairs files, National Archives of Canada.

[17] There are numerous books on Gorbachev, one of which is interesting and useful by the author Robert G.Kaiser, *Why Gorbachev Happened*, Simon & Schuster, Toronto, 1991.

IX. FREE AT LAST

The saga of the growing independence of the communist satellites has been related throughout this monograph. Beginning with Tito's daring break with Stalin in 1949 there were constant attempts by the Soviet satellites to wiggle out concessions from their communist overlords. Some of the countries such as East Germany, Poland, Czechoslovakia and Hungary encountered stiff resistance in their quest for more freedom and independence. Although Khrushchev denounced the brutality of Stalin, he was unwilling to provide any more freedom to his people than his predecessor when he was the secretary general of the Communist Party of the Soviet Union. Brezhnev adopted cautious domestic and foreign policies. This stalemate continued under his successors, Constantine Chernenko and Yuri Andropov. The once powerful state was facing serious political, economic and social problems. An energetic and a wise reformer was needed. Mikhail Gorbachev chosen in 1985 was the man.

The new secretary general of the Communist Party of the Soviet Union lost no time in addressing the problems facing his country and suggesting some solutions. In his speech to the Communist Party he stated that most of the major problems the Soviet Union faced could be solved by economic, political and social restructuring (*perestroika*) and by openness to new ideas and approaches (*glasnost*). He maintained that the "sacred cows" like the leading role of the Communist Party had to be abandoned if reforms were to be effective; more freedom needed to be given to various enterprises and the freedom of the press and speech be encouraged. It did not take long for the press to express opinions on the state of the economy and the need for change. For the first time since the Bolshevik Revolution the communist press covered such topics as prostitution, mismanagement, corruption and minority problems.

Gorbachev then tried to sell his ideas of reform to the satellites. That undertaking was not easy, for most of the communist states except Poland and Hungary had grave reservations as to the effectiveness of his reforms. Even General Jaruzelski gave only a conditional support to the Soviet leader's reforms, for he wanted to wait and see whether the proposed changes would take place in the Soviet Union before committing himself. Hungary already had many evidences of "structuring" and some evidence of "glasnost." Yugoslavia followed its own type of reforms rather than Gorbachev's. Romania and Czechoslovakia were not too enthusiastic about the reforms. Imre Ceausescu, leader of Romania labeled Gorbachev's reforms as "contrary to scientific socialism." The Czech leader, Gustav Husak, was afraid that the reforms would result in another "Prague Spring." Fortunately, Czechoslovakia had a strong industrial basis, which provided a modicum of prosperity without the proposed reforms.

Bulgaria was historically and traditionally tied to the Soviet Union. However, when it came to Gorbachev's reforms the secretary general of the Bulgarian Communist Party, Todar Zhivkov, was rather hesitant to heed the Soviet leader's suggestions. However, after Gorbachev's visit to Bulgaria relations between the two countries improved considerably.

Some of the Soviet satellites did have pragmatic and enterprising leaders. In Czechoslovakia Alexander Dubcek introduced far-reaching economic and political reforms in 1968 only to be stifled by the Soviet masters. Hungary under Janos Kadar (1956-1988) enjoyed a mixed socialist-capitalist economy. From the time he came into power in 1965 Nicolae Ceausescu of Romania began to build up a Stalinist independent state. Although a close adherent of the communist tenets he followed an independent foreign policy. For instance, he did not participate in the Soviet-led invasion of Czechoslovakia in 1968.

Poland was a consistent maverick satellite. Supported by the Roman Catholic Church, a courageous outspoken circle of intellectuals, like Jack Kuron and Adam Michnik, and fearless workers Poland led other communist states in their quest for meaningful political, social and economic reforms. More than any other East European state, Poland waited for the moment when the communist regimes shackles would gradually be removed. Such opportunity occurred in 1980s when the Solidarity Movement pressed for reforms. However, encouraged by the Soviet Union, the Polish leader General Wojech Jaruszelski, imposed martial law, jailed many of the Solidarity leaders and dissolved their association. This law was lifted in 1983 as limited amnesty was extended to those who were incarcerated by the regime.

Events began to move rapidly in Poland. Poles were not satisfied with partial democracy; they wanted democracy with all its trimmings. In June 1989 the first post-World War II elections were held in Poland. Solidarity and independent candidates won all the seats to the Polish parliament (Sejm) and Tadeusz Mazowiecki, a former Solidarity supporter, was chosen prime minister. The transition period was difficult for most of the elected members had little or no experience in governance.[1] Many of the civil servants were recruited from previous communist regimes.

There were other difficulties; productivity declined and inflation increased. The president, Lech Walesa, was not familiar with the workings of a democratic government. He attempted to use his presidential powers without proper consultation with the senate and the sejm. At times he even interfered with the delicate relationship between the legislative and administrative bodies.[2]

Canada was carefully monitoring the events that transpired in Poland. At a dinner on May 8, 1989, hosted by Canada in honour of the Polish foreign minister, Tadeusz Olechowski, the secretary of state for External Affairs, Joe Clark, expressed his satisfaction at the progress made by Poland in the past months. "The appointment of a prominent Solidarity advisor, Tadeusz Mazowiecki," he said, "embodies the reality of political reforms and the acceptance of pluralism in Poland. Canadians applauded this important milestone, the first step towards a representative government reflecting the will of the people. We hope the democratic momentum in Poland continues to unfold." [3]

Canada provided evidence of her intention to foster changes in Poland. Following a warm welcome accorded Lech Walesa during his four-day visit to Canada (November 10-14) 1991 Canada pledged $72 million dollars to assist a process of stabilization of democratic governments in Poland and Hungary.[4] Although this was far short of the amount these countries needed, it was a welcome help keeping in mind the financial plight of both countries. To keep Canada's contribution in proper perspective, Canada also committed help to Eastern Europe through the European Bank for Reconstruction and Development (FBRD) and through an established Task Force, which studied other measures, that Canada could take to assist Eastern Europe.[5]

Events in Central and Eastern Europe moved so rapidly that the Canadian government had difficulty following them. For instance, on February 24, 1989 Joe Clark dispatched a letter to the existing communist regime in Prague protesting the jailing of the human rights activist and Czech play writer, Vaclav Havel. Ten months later the same Clark congratulated Havel in his election as president of Czechoslovakia.

In his New Year's address to the Czechoslovaks, Havel outlined the roadblocks to freedom and prosperity challenging his people to meet them.[6] He was proud of the so-called "velvet" revolution that eventually led to the founding of the Civic Forum, a democratic "think tank." Canada enthusiastically welcomed Havel when he visited Ottawa on February 18 and 19, 1990.

Canada showed a considerable patience with the leaders slow march to democracy but did not tolerate violence in any shape or form. For instance Ottawa was horrified by the "brutal" massacre of civilians by the government police in the Romanian town of Timisoara where a peaceful demonstration ended in violence. Canada announced on December 21, 1989 that she was prepared to impose sanctions on Romania. This was not necessary because the perpetrator of the massacres, Nicolae Ceausescu, and his wife were executed by the mob.[7]

The Role of Mikhail Gorbachev

Canada and Western countries realized that meaningful and permanent changes in Eastern Europe could only occur with the consent and co-operation of the Soviet Union. History attests to the futility and danger of instigating or engaging in a revolt against communist regimes. Canada was convinced that economic, social and political changes must come from the "top." Eastern Europe and the Soviet Union were ripe for significant changes as the Helsinki Accords provided legitimacy for the struggle for human rights and freedoms.

Gorbachev realized that the Soviet Union urgently needed fundamental political, economic and social changes if it were to survive. He articulated his ideas in his two principles of *perestroika* and *glasnost.* He felt that through the implementation of these two principles the Soviet Union could remain communist and at the same time meet the aspirations of the people of the Soviet Union and of Eastern Europe. From the time of his selection as the head of the Soviet Union in 1985 Gorbachev worked hard to achieve his objectives.

The people in East and Central Europe wanted complete independence from the control of Moscow. Gorbachev saw the writing on the wall and gave these people the choice to either remain satellites of Moscow or become free. He assured them that neither the Red Army nor the secret police would interfere with their aspirations for independence. At the same time he hoped that the communist states, once independent, would continue to be friendly to their former master.

Canada was delighted to observe the progress Eastern Europe and the Soviet Union had made towards freedom and democracy. Ottawa fully realized the role Gorbachev played. In his visit to the Soviet Union in November 1989. Prime Minister Brian Mulroney praised Gorbachev for his part in the Soviet reforms. Both heads of state signed fourteen bilateral agreements covering "such areas as peaceful uses of nuclear energy, management of the Arctic and protection of the environment..." The Toronto *Globe and Mail* (November 1989) commented on these new agreements, terming them as sweeping and very helpful in East-West relations. Pleased with what he saw and heard in the Soviet Union, Mulroney quipped that the Cold War was dead and that he was waiting for " the funeral."

Not only was the Cold War dead and buried but the Soviet Union itself was gasping for her life. Gorbachev had many opponents to his vision of the new Soviet Union. Unfortunately he faced a *coup* from his own party members and a movement for independence from the republics. He survived the arrest and attempted *coup*, but he was unable to revive the old Soviet Union. By the end of 1991 USSR was dissolved and republics were invited to join the Commonwealth of Independent States (CIS). The president of the Russian Republic, Boris Yeltsin, signed the Minsk Agreement dissolving the Soviet Union. On Christmas Day, 1991 Gorbachev resigned his position as head of the Soviet Union. The Baltic states of Lithuania, Latvia and Estonia expressed their desire for independence but experienced resistance in their quest for independence from the Soviet Union. The movement for independence could not be stopped. The Baltic States along with Armenia, Georgia, Moldavia and Ukraine gained their independence from the Soviet Union by 1991.

Canada's position was clear; she approved the movement towards independence if the majority of the people wanted it. However, she condemned violence that occurred in Lithuania and Latvia. In January 1991 the minister for External Affairs issued a statement deploring "the use of force against the democratically elected government and the people of Lithuania."[8] In addition, the House of Commons passed a resolution condemning the Soviet military crackdown in the Baltic States, which, in its opinion, violated the Helsinki Accords and the terms of the Paris Peace Treaty signed by major powers in 1949. Ten days later the department for External Affairs also condemned the on-going violence in Latvia initiated by Soviet armed forces.[9]

Canada Offers Assistance to East European States

On May 26, 1990, Joe Clark, the secretary of state for External Affairs, set out the Canadian interests in Europe. Canada was vitally interested in maintaining world peace; in increasing economic links with Europe, be it Eastern or Western; in enhancing existing democratic values present in Europe and in joining Europeans in their battle against global problems. The current Europe according to Clark required a new direction for NATO, an expanded role of CSCE and an intensified relationship with the European Economic Community.

Canada agreed to help Poland get on her feet by offering to wipe out her $40 million debt and guaranteeing $30 million dollars for Canadian investors who wished to develop the East European economy. Some of the money was earmarked for such areas as improvement of agriculture, privatization of assets, important skills in law enforcement, training in fiscal management, telecommunication and preservation of environment. All these innovations were aimed at making democracy secure in Eastern Europe.[10] Other countries in Eastern Europe were not forgotten. Canada promised to send all-party observers to monitor elections in Romania. She contributed $225,000 to assist Czechoslovakia conduct a democratic elections. Altogether Canada agreed to commit $60 million dollars over a period of three years to help East Europeans strengthen their fledging institutions.

Problems in Yugoslavia

Whereas progress was being made peacefully in the development of democratic governments in most of the former communist states, Yugoslavia got unfortunately enveloped in a civil war. When the Serbian "authoritarian fist" in Yugoslavia was lifted, Macedonia, Slovenia and Croatia expressed their desire to become independent. On January 25, 1991 Macedonia opted for independence followed by Slovenia and Croatia on June 25, 1991. Without waiting for a recommendation from the United Nations, Germany recognized the independence of Slovenia and Croatia. Serbia was not willing to witness the disintegration of Yugoslavia and began to using her National Army to subdue the independence movement. The Croatian army was no match for the Serbian forces who were well equipped and well trained. Right from the beginning the war had the characteristics of a blood bath and neither side took steps to end the conflict.

The United Nations did its level best to negotiate a settlement but with little success. The new Canadian secretary of state for External Affairs, Barbara McDougall, strongly urged all parties involved "to seek a resolution to the constitutional problems" and to refrain from using force. She supported the use of the office of the Conference on Security and Cooperation in Europe to settle the problem. "In our view," she stated," "the Yugoslav crisis poses not only a human tragedy of enormous proportion but also a direct threat to international peace." [11]

When the request to observe a cease-fire did not seem to go anywhere the European Community decided to impose sanctions on the warring parties. Violence and atrocities continued. Thereupon, the United Nations sent a peacekeeping force to restore and maintain peace in this region. The maintenance of the United Nations' forces in Yugoslavia for the last fifteen years confirms the necessity to have such a UN presence in Yugoslavia in the first place.

Changes in Military Alliances

With the achievement of independence of communist satellites and the demise of the Soviet Union both the Russians and the NATO allies raised a number of questions. Was it necessary to have military alliances? If so, what would the function of these alliances be? How could the world be assured that nuclear weapons in the independent republics were safely stored and carefully monitored?

Representatives of six East European nations met in Budapest on November 15, 1990 and agreed to withdraw from the Warsaw Treaty Organization, thus giving direct a deathblow to it. Some of the six members entertained the possibility of joining NATO. To add to the existing confusion and uncertainty some NATO partners did not advocate the abolition of their military alliance but agreed to re-consider its role in the light of the unprecedented changes in the Soviet Union and Eastern Europe. All attempts were being made to co-operate with the Soviet Union and her former satellites. The sixteen members of NATO met in London, England and came out with a Declaration on the Transformed North Atlantic Alliance:

We recognize," began the statement, "that in the new Europe, the security of every state is inseparably linked to the security of its neighbours. NATO must become an institution where Europeans, Canadians and Americans work together, not only for the common defence, but (also) for building new partnerships with all the nations of Europe. The Atlantic Community must reach out to the countries of the East, which were our adversaries in the Cold War, and extend to them the hand of friendship." [12]

Notes

[1] Wlodzimierz Wesolowski, "Transition from Authoritarianism to Democracy," *Eastern Europe*, edited by Lyman H. Legters, D.C. Heath Co., 1992, Toronto, pp. 300-316.

[2] Jan B. Weydental, "The First Hundred Days of Walesa's Presidency," edited by Lyman H. Ledgers, *ibid.* pp. 336-339.

[3] Remarks Joe Clark made at the dinner on May 8, 1989, *Statements and Speeches,* Department for External Affairs, (hereafter noted as DEA) National Archives of Canada.

[4] *Ibid., p.* 104.

[5] *Ibid.*, p. 105

[6] Address by President Vaclav Havel to the Czechoslovak nation, January 1, 1991, *Eastern Europe*, edited by Lyman H. Legters, *op. cit.*, pp. 371-376.

[7] Vladimir Tismaneanu, "In Romania: Between Euphoria and Rage," found in *Eastern Europe, ibid.* pp.467-473.

[8] *News Release,* by the secretary of state for External Affairs, National Archives of Canada.

[9] *News Release,* January 21, 1991, *ibid.*

[10] *Statements and Speeches,* department for External Affairs, May 26, 1990.

[11] Statement made by Barbara MacDougall in the House of Commons during an emergency debate on the situation in Yugoslavia, November 18, 1991. See *The Debates of the House of Commons,* 1991.

[12] *Annual Review of Politics and Public Affairs, 1990*, edited by David Leyton Brown, University of Toronto Press, pp. 99-100.

AUTHOR'S INTERVIEWS OF CANADIAN DIPLOMATS

Blanchette, Arthur
Ford, Robert
Hart, Albert
Holmes, John
Ignatieff, George
McCordick, Jack
Pickersgill, Jack
Rogers, Benjamin
Seaborn, Ben
Smith, Arnold
Southam, Hamilton

Introduction

Appendices are useful tools in many ways. They provide an avenue where materials, pertinent as they may be, are better located outside the text. In that way the narrative flow is not interrupted. The contents of the interviews with the diplomats become their "mouth pieces" or their authentic "voices" relating their successes, frustrations and experiences which in many cases would remain in dusty records of the Canadian Foreign Office. Even though there might be some repetition in the dialogues of those interviewed, the interest engendered by the stories and experiences far out weigh the benefits of repetitions. In many cases the interviews become part of a "detective narration" sustaining the readers' curiosity about the work and the lives of individuals who represented Canada.

Each diplomatic officer sent to serve in a foreign post receives a set of "instructions." From time to time some government officials and even the public questioned the utility of diplomats particularly during the Cold War period when trade was minimal and immigration and cultural exchanges practically non-existent. Without the diplomats in the Soviet Union beginning during the War and somewhat later in Poland, Czechoslovakia and Yugoslavia Canada would not have an appraisal of what was going on behind the

Iron Curtain. The copious documents sent to Ottawa by the Canadian ambassador Lana Wilgress provided vital information about the Soviet Union and her foreign policy. His work was continued by another able diplomat, Robert Ford. The diplomatic service formed the "eyes and the ears" of the government abroad. At the same time it protected Canadian citizens in case of harassment and were "on the spot" to evaluate situations....

Since contacts with the general public were carefully watched and the media controlled by the state it was difficult to obtain information about Eastern Europe. Meeting government officials in social gathering proved at times a fruitful manner of procuring information and analysis. In time the diplomats learned to "read between the lines", that is not what government is not seen in the newspaper, or on television. Canadian diplomats cultivated close relationship with the Americans, British, and Australians and from time to time with representatives from India. Although Canadian Foreign Service was small compared with the Americans and the British, yet in quality it was considered as one of best in terms of its efficiency and service. The rigorous entrance qualification and continuous upgrading of skills made the Canadian Foreign Service the envy of many countries.

Posts in the Soviet Union and Eastern Europe were considered as "hardship posts" The amenities enjoyed in the Western countries were, generally, not found in the Eastern bloc countries. However, Canadian diplomats accommodated themselves with regards to meals, travel and entertainment. Some of them took short jaunts to Switzerland or Sweden to break down the monotony associated with their assignment. Particularly the wives of the diplomats welcomed trips abroad many of them found their stay challenging, to say the least. Some diplomats like Robert Ford, developed respect for the Russian culture and literature and others like Southam Hamilton, Albert Hart and Jack McCordick admired Polish culture. Some of the Canadian representatives, namely Ford, Arnold Smith and John Holmes were recognized for their analysis of the Canadian foreign policy dealing with communist countries.

During the "détente" Canada through her contacts with Soviet and East European officials involved in trade, cultural exchanges and visits presented them examples of Canadian values in a quiet and unobtrusive way. Canada was committed to "building confidence" between the West and the East.

Arthur Blanchette

Arthur Blanchette whom the author interviewed on June 19, 1984, was never posted in any of the East European countries but he did have indirect connections with one or more of these countries by being involved with the Canadian Information Service and later with CBC-IS (Canadian Broadcasting Corporation International Service.) The latter beamed information on Canada to the Soviet Union and to Eastern bloc countries. As a member of the Supervisory Commission in Indo-China he had contacts with Polish delegates. His experiences abroad particularly in Mexico, Latin America, and the United States provided him with a broad and penetrating view of world events. He was also appointed as Canada's first representative to the Organization of American States (0AS).

What was your experienced with the Canadian Information Service?

The CIS was amalgamated with the department of External Affairs in 1947. Its basic purpose was to gather information. As an officer of the department I was posted to Mexico in 1948 and had exposure for three years to the politics and culture of Latin America. We weren't trying to sell anything nor were we trying to get them do anything. We were just trying to let them know what we were doing and to maintain friendly relations.

I came back to the International Service in the late 1959 and I noticed a considerable change in the overall outlook of this organization. During my first stint with the Service every thing was fine. There was an attempt to present Canada in the best possible light. During the War we were trying to persuade the Germans that their regime was not the best in the world. About ten years later I found the same sort of reaction we had with the Russians.

When I returned from Cambodia in 1959 where I was made the head of the liaison division, "détente" was beginning. However, in the International service the Cold War atmosphere seemed to hang on. In part it was because of the staff we had hired. Many members of the staff were refugees from Eastern Europe who harboured memories of oppression. One of the main tasks of CIS was to have the messages of the staff toned down. Although I was one of the spokesmen there was also in the Department of External Affairs a psychological warfare committee.

What was your approach towards Eastern Europe?

We thought that probably the best approach to Eastern Europe would be to let facts in Canada speak for themselves. For instance, if Canada had a good grain crop or if we were producing many automobiles, we would say so instead of saying that the Russians were poor farmers and that their system was terrible because there was insufficient food to feed the Russian people. We felt that during this time of détente the Russians could reach their own conclusions.

Was there resistance to this approach?

Yes, indeed. There was a good deal of soul- searching going on not only in the department of External Affairs but also in the Treasury Board. We were constantly asking the question whether the CIS should be maintained considering the cost of operating it. Norman Robertson and L.B. Pearson were for it whereas others were not. Instead of bringing the issue to the cabinet Pearson just left it alone. Perhaps this saved the International Service.

When I returned to Ottawa in 1968 the International Service was what it is to day; there was a budget from the CBC and the National Service Commission. The size of the staff was curtailed as many languages disappeared. New programs were initiated.

Why was Sackville New Brunswick chosen as the cite for the towers?

Sackville was chosen after very intense study. It is one of the areas in Canada, which is suited climatically, meteorologically and geologically. There are very few spots in the world like that in the world. Another such spot is in the French Congo where radio short-wave transmission is excellent. Recently the CIS has been given more powerful transmitters and a new role to play; a cultural one.

Could you tell me how did you perceive yourself as a Canadian diplomat?

Clearly every diplomat was sent abroad for a number of reasons. Most importantly he was asked to represent Canadian interests abroad, to protect Canadians, and to develop Canadian interests. But we also had as a part of our mandate to present a favourable image of Canada to the local population, and to show how good Canada is. I did this in Indonesia and everywhere else I have been. In my opinion as a diplomat should maintain a sort of a sympathetic understanding of the problems encountered by the local population, along with their cherished aspirations, and their ideals.

What was the nature of the instructions you received when you were sent abroad?

When I reached Indonesia I received instructions one of which was to increase trade between Canada and the country where I was sent. The Canadian government wanted each diplomat to do everything possible to create jobs and to foster industrial production. Things change rapidly. For instance CIDA is now not only an aid dispensing arm of the Canadian government but is also a credit dispensing agent of the Canadian government. What are priorities now in Eastern Europe may not be so in years to come.

Robert D. Ford

As one of the predecessors of Lana Wilgress Ford became an expert on Soviet Union spending twenty-one years in that country and twenty years, 1964 to 1980 as Canadian ambassador in Moscow. Besides his distinguished career in the Foreign Service, he was also a noted poet publishing some seven volumes of poetry most of them in the Russian language. From 1959 to 1961 he was Canadian ambassador to Yugoslavia. The author interviewed Ford in Ottawa in November 1984.

What was it like to be in Yugoslavia in 1960s?

It was extremely important for Canada to maintain a legation in Yugoslavia. From this post Canada was able to glean information about other East European countries and about the Soviet Union. Trade and tourism were also important reasons for cultivating relations with Yugoslavia. Ethnic groups particularly the Croats were of some concern to Canadians.

You were in Moscow when the Soviet-led invasion of Czechoslovakia occurred. What was your feeling about this invasion?

I always felt that whoever controlled the Bohemian region controlled Central Europe. Brezhnev and the East Germans were very uneasy about the liberalization that was occurring under Dubcek. And there was a feeling that if this was allowed to happen other countries might try this in their own country. I am rather convinced the Russians were not interested in extending their territories but at the same time they did not appreciate anyone challenging their right to Eastern Europe.

Out of the six East European countries which countries did Canada have a certain preference.

Poland was preferred for number of reasons. It was the first of the countries that became a victim of Hitler's aggression and later of Soviets manipulation. Canadians and Poles fought side by side in the Second World War. There were a large number of Canadians who could trace their racial origin to Poland. In general Canadians appreciated Polish culture.

After making the comments on the Poles I could say about the same thing about the Czechoslovaks. The two founders of Czechoslovakia, Thomas Masaryk and Eduard Benes were highly respected by most Canadians. There was always a feeling that Czechoslovakia had the most successful democratic government of all East European countries.

Since you served as a Canadian diplomat in the Soviet Union and in Yugoslavia and you also served in posts in the West, what were the differences between Western and Eastern posts?

Posts in Eastern Europe were totally different from those in the West. Housing, standard of living, and facilities greatly varied in quality and in quantity. There was a significant difference between Moscow and Belgrade. There were fewer restrictions in Yugoslavia than in the Soviet Union. From the social point of view I found the Yugoslavs friendlier than the Russians.

What type of preparation does one need to be effective in the Civil Service? Eastern Europe?

Generally speaking the department of External Affairs could send almost anyone to Western posts because the quality of life is fairly the same in Western countries. But it would not be wise to send unprepared personnel to the Soviet Union and Eastern Europe. These diplomats had to have special training and be of certain disposition. For most part East European posts were hardship posts where the language and traditions were different from what most people experienced in the West.

What contacts did you have with the Russians when you were an ambassador?

I had frequent contacts with Russian poets and writers that provided me with valuable information. Since I possessed a thorough knowledge of the Russian language I could interpret better the workings of the Soviet mind. I had the opportunity of meeting many Russian government officials and people during the time of Khrushchev. There was little contact with the people and even with the members of the government during the time of Brezhnev. In general many of the intellectuals identified themselves quite closely with the West.

What else would you, Mr. Ford, add about the Soviet Union and Eastern Europe?

In my experience professional Marxists continued to believe in the communist doctrine. The average Soviet citizen was taught that Marxism would spread throughout the whole world and that in time the Soviet Union would conquer the world. However, the men and women on the street, in the factory or on their kolkhozes were more pragmatic. They wanted a decent living for themselves and for their children. In the Soviet satellites there existed an atmosphere of hostility towards Moscow and what it represented.

Albert F. Hart

Albert F. Hart was interviewed by the author on May 6, 1984. He served in Belgrade, Moscow, and Berlin and in Warsaw. He served two terms in Poland first in 1951and then as an ambassador in 1971. His colleagues regarded his perception of Eastern Europe and particularly of East Berlin with respect. He studied Marxism at Harvard University.

How did you find Warsaw when you came in 1951?

It was really a very grim place indeed. Life was pretty difficult. The city was still, in 1951 half destroyed; reconstruction had made tremendous strides, the people were very hard working and, of course being such great patriots, they were dedicated to the idea of rebuilding their city as quickly as possible. The reconstruction process was so intense that even on a nice summer day there would be kind of a haze of dust overlying the city. This of course the first year of what we might call intensive sovietization and the first year of the first year of the Six Five Plans of accelerated industrialization.

It wasn't purely industrialization because it was also the beginning of armament, for Stalin wanted Poland to become the second largest military power in Eastern Europe. Thirty percent of the Six Five Year Plan was devoted to the military industry. Most of the money was spent on armament and very little on consumer goods. Unfortunately the living conditions of the average Pole were pretty dreadful.

When you first came to Poland where did you live?

We lived in a quite nice apartment that my predecessor, Bill Foote, was able to get. We had only two officers and that was enough for we did not have much to do. During the whole year we might have had ten visitors from Canada most of them being members of the Royal Peace Consulate. They would come and sample our Canadian whiskey and then launch into a glorious support of communist regimes.

Since we did not have any emigration from Poland and precious little trade why did we have a legation in Poland?

At one point of time Ottawa was considering closing posts in Poland and Czechoslovakia. If one looked at the kind of work I was able to do in the first year of my appointment one could say that there was little value in having the post opened. We had the problem of the Polish Art Treasures hanging around our neck, but I do not think that was the reason for keeping the legation opened. And Poland was a satellite state doing what Moscow wanted her to do.

The reason why we kept a legation opened goes back to war years when Poland established a government-in-exile in London, England and Canada established diplomatic relations with Poland. Poles contributed significantly to the victory over Germany. Now it was but normal course of events that when Poland was liberated relations would continue. Very few people thought that Poland would become a communist state. We, Canadians, were a bit naïve those days, for we thought that there would be a free election in Poland as Stalin promised at the Yalta conference. The allies including Canada were terribly disappointed when this did not come about.

We recognized the Provisional Government of National Unity on July 5, 1945 and we withdrew our recognition of the Polish government-in-exile. We treaded a very delicate path being sympathetic, on one hand to the Polish-government-in-exile and on the other hand we were carrying business with the government in Warsaw little as it was.

Since you were in Belgrade and Warsaw how do these two posts differ from each other?

There were outstanding differences. It is true that there is strong nationalism demonstrated in both countries but there are different ways people express it. Tito of Yugoslavia took a stand against Stalin and succeeded because he had the people behind him. He had an advantage over Houlka, the Polish leader, because he achieved victory over the Germans without the assistance of Moscow. In Yugoslavia the communist party was largely home grown whereas in Poland the original party was destroyed and later restored by Stalin. Communism in Poland was imposed upon the people.

However, communist rule in both countries was rigid, regimental leaving little room for democratic rights.

Were Canada's feelings towards Yugoslavia the same as the feelings towards Poland?

Well, I wouldn't say that they were the same. Canada had always a close cultural and religious respect for the Polish people. Most of the Polish people who immigrated to Canada became good citizens. The number of Yugoslavs who emigrated from the area that is now called Yugoslavia was relatively small. Roman Catholicism was a powerful link between Canada and Poland. There were other aspects of European culture that we as Canadians share with the Poles. Because some of Yugoslavia had been under Turkish rule for many years the traditions and customs of Bosnians and Herzogovinians were quite different from those of Canadians.

Was the volume of Yugoslavia trade with Canada greater than the Polish trade with Canada?

Of course, Canada had a larger volume of trade with Poland than with Yugoslavia. I remember a Yugoslav delegation that came to Canada to discuss the purchase of high-bred seed corn. Yugoslavs also wanted to sell to Canada baby chicks and small potatoes. We need to keep in mind that the East European bloc countries, under the leadership of Stalin, refused to trade with Yugoslavia as a result of the rupture of 1949. Unexpected drought and the drive towards collectivization made it difficult for the people of Yugoslavia.

Americans were very generous in their help not only in food but also in military equipment. United States was a favorite trading partner of Yugoslavia. Yugoslavia was also interested in maintaining its military forces in case they were attacked by the Soviet Union.

You were in Warsaw and Belgrade during the height of the Cold War. How were you able to glean valuable information on the Soviet Union and Eastern Europe?

Yes, it was difficult to get information. Well, we did get out among the people, by taking a weekend trips. If you were driving a car there was always someone who needed a lift. This provided an occasion to strike a conversation. And even on trains one could engage in conversation while others were talking loud enough to drown what we were talking about. One thing was certain I as a diplomat visited the Polish Foreign Ministry five or six time during my two and half years in Poland. During the years 1951-53 we were not invited by the Ministry often. The Cold War was on.

I understand that you were in Budapest during the Hungarian Revolution. What happened?

Well, I got caught at the outbreak of the crisis as we were traveling to Vienna to attend a wheat conference. My wife and I decided to spend the night in Budapest and go to an opera. We arrived in the city just an hour before the Revolution started. The streets were crowded and people were marching up and down. We had difficulty in getting a hotel. We got a hotel on the Marquette Island but found it difficult to leave the island for all the roads were blocked by the Red Army.

The next morning all hell let loose. We had to lie low for five days and then we joined a convoy with white flags. But hoisting the white flag did not help us much because we had to pass through a cordon of freedom fighter. When the fighters saw a red star of Belgrade on the car license plate they wanted to take us into the woods and dispose the car and us. Fortunately there were some people who assured these freedom fighters that we were harmless. Further down the road we came across the Red Army who looked very ominous. All I can say is that it was an exciting but a frightening experience.

You were also in Moscow when Khrushchev was in power. What was your perception of Moscow?

Well, you certainly felt like you were at the center of power. You might say that power radiated from Moscow to the whole area of Europe and perhaps found its countervailing force when the Russians met the American power. It was very interesting period because things changed very rapidly. Khrushchev continued to go on tangents. When he ran against a brick wall at the end of the tangent he turned to another tangent. Whether the tangents were concerned with internal affairs or foreign affairs they all seemed to run into a stone wall; eventually he got stuck.

Compare and contrast security in the countries you worked.

In the Soviet Union you had to get a written permission to travel 25 km or more from Moscow. In Poland you did not need such permission. However, you were followed. It became rather tedious for the security who attempted to follow us all the time. If you stopped for an outside picnic there were" those fellows." In Russia these security officers drove old cetroline cars at about 60 miles an hour having exhaust from the car smoke to "beat the band." I always felt that all this surveillance was a waste of time and natural resources. In order to pass our time while traveling in we decided to count the number of red haired Poles we passed or saw.

Did Canada consider her relationship with Eastern Europe marginal?

Well, I certainly would not say it was marginal. But you have to make a distinction between the feelings of the people and the feelings of the government. If you want to promote good relations between the people of Canada and say the people of Poland or Ukraine you have to somehow or other bring the governments into the picture. Our approach was to work with the governments for we did feel that we had certain common interests with those governments. After all, despite their different ideologies these governments had concern for the welfare of their people.

One of the forces that united people was their national and cultural aspiration. We have to keep in mind that the super powers like the Soviet

Union and the United States have slightly different concerns. Smaller nations like Canada want to cultivate peaceful relations with her neighbours. They want to promote the development of their respective countries through co-operation. It seems to me that we were too concerned with developing friendly relations with the Soviet Union and neglecting the development of relations with such smaller countries as Poland and Yugoslavia. Smaller countries could restrain the larger and more powerful ones.

Did the Canadian government ever use Poland and Yugoslavia as a counter weight against Soviet domination?

No, I do not think so. That would be very risky. And we realized that as early as 1956 at the time of the Hungarian Revolution that precious little could be done to restrain a major power. Intervening in the Revolution would have made things worse. Stirring trouble between the Russians and the Poles and between the Yugoslavs and the Russians makes no progress. What one hopes to see are significant changes in the Soviet Union which in turn would affect Eastern Europe.

Were Canadians in general and Canadian diplomats in particular trusted more than the Americans or the Russians?

I think that people felt more relaxed in our company because we were members of a small country and therefore could operate in a slightly friendlier atmosphere. But that does not mean that we received more information than the Americans. There were however exceptions; we did get useful information during the Hungarian Revolution and the in the 1975 when I became the Canadian ambassador to Poland.

In contrast to my first appointment in 195I I observed a tremendous change in the attitude of the people in 1971 when I became the Canadian ambassador to Poland. Everybody was friendly. It was a type of a honeymoon in our relations with Poland. There were numerous projects considered and some developed. The tremendous activity underscores the importance of developing relations with Eastern European countries.

Some of the documents I saw indicated that the Poles were considered business-like and competent in negotiations. Could you comment?

If you consider the Polish diplomatic service in Canada it was quite strong with commercial offices in Toronto and Montreal. Poland had people with the export organization who traveled across Canada. When you speak to these individuals, as I have done, you discover how knowledgeable they were. In fact they were sometimes more knowledgeable than the Canadian business-men. They worked at their tasks and were very hospitable. Their soup, called *borst*, was heavenly.

What other comments do you wish to make?

Poles have values and keep these afloat in times of great adversity. These values helped them to survive as individuals and as a nation. On one occasion the Pope said that "it was easier for a Pole or a Russian to find God in their societies than it was for one living in a capitalist state." In his opinion we have become too materialistic.

John W. Holmes

John Holmes was one of the most perceptive analysts of Canadian foreign policy Canada ever had. His humble and gentle manners concealed his critical intellect and his penetrating power of discernment. He frequently took a back stage position patiently waiting for an opportunity to add pearls of wisdom on a given issue. A graduate of the University of Toronto he joined the department of External Affairs during the War and served in Moscow for nine months. Most of his energy and insights were dedicated to the effective operation of the United Nations where he was frequently one of Canada's representatives. The author interviewed him on November 28, 1984.

In what way did the Canadian foreign policy towards Eastern Europe consistent with the events that transpired in Europe?

I think that it differed considerably in that we took for granted that the East European countries followed blindly the dictates of the Kremlin. In many cases this was true but in other cases it was not. Take for instance the independent stance Yugoslavia and Romania took. And even Poland under the leadership of Wladyslaw Gomulka initiated in 1956 what at that time was called "the Polish path to socialism." The Polish foreign minister Adam Rapacki in 1960s tried his utmost to bring about the creation of a demilitarized zone between East Germany and Poland.

What happened to this plan?

The Soviet Union and the West for different reasons opposed it. However, it succeeded in another way; it encouraged the movement towards détente, inviting them to speak with one another rather than scream at each other. East European desperately wanted détente as they recognized that the reduction of tensions would be of great benefit to them. Canada did not have any difficulty in recognizing East Germany and quietly recommended this on the Western powers. Besides East Germany, Bulgaria and Czechoslovakia were opposed to détente.

What was the position of Yugoslavia in the 1960s?

It belonged to the non-aligned nations after breaking ties with the Soviet Union. This did not make them more acceptable to Canadians who were unwilling to forgive Tito's persecution of the Catholic Church nor his record of violation of human rights. On the official level we had correct relations with Yugoslavia particularly in the United Nations.

Some of the more significant moves were initiated in the United Nations. For example the solution for the detention of the Polish Art Treasures occurred at this world organization. I had very useful conversations with the Polish representative Mumford Lachs. As a result of these informal talks the solution to the release of the first consignment of Art Treasures stored in the Bank of Montreal took place.

Were there any restrictions of travel in the Soviet Union and in Eastern Europe?

From experience I know that there were restrictions in the Soviet Union. One could not travel beyond 25 kilometers of the place one stayed without authorization from the Kremlin. There were no such restrictions in Poland; however, Canadians were carefully followed when they traveled. Canada placed the same mile restrictions on the Russians when they came to Canada but they were usually waived.

How did the British government assist Canada in Hungary?

During the Hungarian revolution the British government offered to look after Canadian interests in the absence of Canadian diplomats. This task became rather onerous as thousands of Hungarian refugees wished to enter Canada and those who had already entered, wanted to contact their relatives. The British overwhelmed with the work of processing refugees, asked Canada to help their officers. This Canada did by posting an official in Budapest to cope with the situation.

What is your assessment of Canadian legations in Eastern Europe?

In general the personnel in Canadian legations were very good even though we did not have enough East European experts. There were times we used retired generals and political leaders. For the most part these did acceptable service. We did not want to use Canadians of East European extraction in case the regimes could hold the families of the of these professionals as bargaining options for certain favours. There were occasions when we did post Canadians in Eastern Europe who had language facilities.

Did Canadian diplomats help formulate Canadian foreign policy?

Certainly particularly when it came to Canada's policy towards the Soviet Union. In the persons of Dana Wilgress and Robert Ford Canada had two of the most knowledgeable experts of Canadian-Soviet relations. Dispatches of Wilgress sent to the department of External Affairs during and after the war formed the basic foundation for Canada's policy towards the Soviet Union. This also can be said of Ford whose vision and longevity in Moscow provided a continuity of the work of Wilgress. They also influenced Canada's relations with Eastern Europe. Political scientists do not always realize how the present technology made it possible to have the government and the members of the legations exchange messages easily.

What do think of American rollback policy?

Canadian officials were always suspicious of the American rollback policy. We would be delighted to drive the communists out of all the East European countries, but we knew from the Hungarian revolution experience that this would have caused a blood bath. Campaign where the citizens of the communist countries would be involved would be a step backward. Just the promise to the people of Eastern Europe liberation using Radio-Free Europe would initiate expectation the allies could not deliver. To some Polish or Czechoslovakian émigrés Canadian objection to the rollback policy appeared as if the allies abandoned them. There was in most Western countries a hope that the new governments would be somewhat to the "left of center." As much we despised Soviet imperialism and the division of the world between the free and the captive world we were not in favour of using force to dislodge the communists.

What do you think would help to eliminate the possibility of another Cold War period?

To begin with, one of the things I blame the Russians for is their secrecy. If they had been more open and more honest with us, I think they would have had our continued sympathy as we demonstrated during the World War II. When I was in Moscow I did not think that the Soviets were about to invade us. But they arouse our suspicions. You couldn't move or do anything. So we got suspicious and did things that made them suspicious of us. These suspicions fueled the Cold War. What we could have done was to initiate a dialogue with them.

Did you have conversations with Igor Gouzenko?

Yes, I did and he used to come to see me under the name of Peter Brown. I thought that I was one of the few people who had the privilege of speaking to him, but I found out later that countless of others spoke to him. Actually he phoned me last night as he was traveling through Toronto.

In your opinion, who were some of the individuals who influenced the Canadian foreign policy?

We had great confidence in the British foreign office. I get angry when I hear that Canada adopted the American attitude towards the Cold War. Like other countries we were trying to listen to other people and then come with our own idea we should adopt during the Cold War. For instance we listened to an Italian ambassador to Moscow who was highly regarded and who knew the Soviet Union well. We also had good relations with the Indians at that time. Actually Russians were treating the Indians a little better than they were treating others. I also had contacts with good press correspondents, some of whom were left wing in politics.

I would attempt to put all the information together to form a picture of what was going on. Of course, George Kennan and the American state department were also very valuable. I also found the Finnish and the Swedish ambassadors helpful in providing me with added insights on Eastern Europe and on the Soviet Union.

To what extent did ethnic groups influence the Canadian foreign policy?

It seems to me that it wasn't so much of the "third group" of Canadians that influenced Canadian foreign policy but it was the perception the political parties had of these groups. Individuals like John Diefenbaker had a glorious dream that there were millions of ethnic votes one could garnish. And yet how many Ukrainian Canadians understood and even less cared to have a for free Ukraine. Large number of Italian and German Canadians did not have much interest in Eastern Europe.

I remember Michael Staar going out of his way trying to persuade ethnic votes by stressing that such a vote, somehow, would help free Ukraine. I had two friends, one Polish and the other Hungarian who though very anti-communist and anti-Russian said that they would not vote for Staar and the Conservative Party because he and his party were exploiting the people. They maintained that there wasn't a thing Staar could do to improve the lot of the people in Hungary and Poland except in a very general sense. And to play on the emotions made these gentlemen angry. I don't blame them. It wasn't a success; it was but an illusion in the minds of many people.

To what extent was the issue of security involved in our relations with Eastern Europe?

We were never certain whether those who asked to be admitted into Canada were not former Nazis or fascists. At the same time we were concerned about admitting communists into the country. Although some of these were fascist collaborators most of them were not.

One of the things that worried me was the number of prisoner-of-war that was sent back to the Soviet Union. To say that most of these were certain of death is, in my opinion, incorrect. Recent information indicates that many were not liquidated. We should have opened the gates to more displaced persons. The standard argument for not having more of these people come to Canada was the lack of transportation. Canada was in a hurry to transport returning members of the armed forces in the years following the end of the war.

There were thousands of starving Germans awaiting an opportunity to enter Canada. We cannot say that the Germans deserved this type of treatment for many were innocent. We were also worried about the treatment Russians would give the prisoners of war.

George Ignatieff

The author interviewed George Ignatieff on November 27, 1984. Ignatiev served Canada in many different capacities. In 1955 he accompanied Lester B. Pearson to the Soviet Union. In 1957 he was appointed the Canadian ambassador to Yugoslavia where he served for two years. On a number of occasions he was the Canadian representative at the United Nations. During the time of Prime Minister Trudeau he worked diligently on the Trudeau Peace Initiative. In the 1980's he served as the Chancellor of the University of Toronto.

What, in your opinion, led to the Cold War?

I believe that the breakdown of negotiations on the use of atomic energy marked the beginning of the Cold War. At the same time Stalin's lack of trust in the allies did not help matters. To be honest, neither side was frank with one another. The Americans tried to keep information about the development of an atomic bomb away from the Russians.

The first sign of direct confrontation was in 1948 when I was a deputy to General McNaughton, Canada's representative at the conference on atomic energy. There was trouble brewing in Iran, Greece and Czechoslovakia. In the latter country the so-called "Brezhnev doctrine" was used to justify the *coup* carried out in 1948. The Soviets took the position that the people of Czechoslovakia wanted a communist government. I was in the chair at that time and I asked the Security Council whether they would agree to have the Czech representative, Dr. Popanik, give his version of the events. After a rather stormy session Popanik was allowed to speak. As the result of the *coup* NATO was formed. One should remember that a year later Tito broke with Stalin over his proposed domination of the Balkan region.

I was sent as an ambassador to Yugoslavia in 1956 and saw first hand how a country could claim to be communist and yet resist being part of the Soviet bloc and be dictated by Moscow. Tito insisted that nationalism should take precedence over communism and be more humanitarian. It was interesting to watch the various experiments he instituted.

Unlike the United States, Canada was not a source of military support for Yugoslavia. We did have an active cultural exchanges and a good deal of trade. We not only sent agriculture experts to Yugoslavia but also set up a branch of Massey Ferguson. We also had a modest student exchange program. Students from the Royal Military College came to Yugoslavia to discover the type of defence a non-aligned country could build. At the time of the Hungarian Revolution some of the freedom fighters escaped to Yugoslavia and from there they came to Canada. This humanitarian move helped Yugoslavia to make the decision to let these Hungarians go to Canada rather than risk the possibility of sending them to prison or even worse, death.

How did the West try to contain the Soviet Union's aggression and expansion?

Our distinguished diplomat, Wilgress, and others shared our view that it was important for NATO to give our partners a sense of confidence so that they would not be overcome or overtaken by the Soviet military power. This sense of solidarity would not allow such countries as West Germany, Italy, Norway or any other county adjacent to the Soviet Union suffer the fate of Czechoslovakia. Such a stand would give the Soviets a signal that an attack on any of these countries would be considered an attack on all of them.

It was inherent in the Canadian foreign policy that NATO, because of Article 2 was more than a military alliance. At the beginning the West depended on the United States having a nuclear deterrent. But this balance changed when the Soviet Union also had a nuclear bomb thus reaching the position of parity. Mr. Pearson and Mr. St. Laurent maintained that NATO could only be "a lasting system of collective security...if it showed solidarity not only in mobilizing military strength but also in common attitude to East-West relations." The question that faced us is what is permissible in this state of "peaceful co-existence". When Pearson went to the Soviet Union in 1955 and I accompanied him we had some trade talks and we emphasized that certain strategic materials such as trucks could not be considered for imports because they could be used militarily. I clearly remember working for hours with Mitchell Sharp on a communiqué in which we stated that in strategic material there could not be included in any trade talks. We were willing to sell grain to the Soviet Union as we did during the tenure of John Diefenbaker. The Americans objected to our sale of grain to communist states. On one occasion the foreign minister of China approached Howard Green, the Canadian minister for Foreign Affairs, and thanked him and Canada for making a distinction between humanitarian aid and adherence to the dictates of an alliance.

If we look at the so-called "communist threat" analytically we note various forces at work in totalitarian states. The Moscow type of totalitarianism does not fit the Chinese, the Vietnamese or Eastern European with all of their divergences. One of the questions that worries me is stressing militarism in our lives for it gives permission for the other sided to do likewise. A good example is Poland where the people wish to regain their freedom and independence by referring to the military threat. In actuality it is not a military threat; it is really a political threat and an economic threat.

When I was on the Security Council there was a debate about the Soviet-led invasion of Czechoslovakia. With all the talk of rollback the Americans shrugged their shoulders and said we can't do anything in this situation. Under the excuse that they were changing their ambassador to the UN they asked me to deliver the Western response. Again we took the line of 1948 *coup*. There was a slight difference for we had Dr. Hagen a spokesman for the Duck to give the response. While waiting for Dr. Hagen to arrive from Belgrade we kept the debate going. When he did arrive he refuted the allegation that the Soviet-led troops were invited to prevent civil war.

Was there a distinct Canadian foreign policy towards Eastern Europe?

I think there was. Canada was far less disposed than the United States to lump all the East European countries into one monolithic communist bowl. Each of these countries reacted differently to Stalin's policy of conquest whereby the East European countries lost their freedom. The Poles were consistently the most reluctant to be embraced by the Russians. In the scale of resistance, Yugoslavs, Romanians and Hungarians came second. Bulgarians because of the historical roots seemed to be willing to follow loyally the Moscow line. I should note that we did not declare war on Bulgaria because she was a friend of the Soviet Union, a country that was our war ally. Canada has developed cultural relations with Poland, Hungary and Yugoslavia.

What do you think of Adam Rapacki's concept of a demilitarized zone between Poland and East Germany?

One of the interesting episodes regarding security was Rapacki's initiative. I was present at the meeting when Howard Green and Adam Rapacki met in Geneva. At that time the Polish foreign minister outlined his plan for disengagement in Central Europe, something in which we were interested in some form or another. I'm sure that it was the key to reducing the risk of a war by accident.

Rapacki held that historically Poland and Germany had been the areas of immediate impact in the event of war and this constantly worried him. Once West Germany was allowed to re-arm there was tremendous pressure on NATO to put forces as near to East Germany as possible. NATO was relying more and more on the nuclear weapons to counter the threat from the Soviet Union's superior armed forces. What worried Poles were the nuclear mines and nuclear ammunitions for various projectiles. Once these go off, and the threshold is crossed, there is bound to be an escalation. This is something that both sides admittedly did not want.

If nuclear short-range weapons were removed, we could then move into de-nuclearization such areas as oceans and air. Canada has shown that some of this could be done. I am told that we have removed the last nuclear warheads from Canada. The same can be done in Europe.

If the Rapacki's Plan was that good why did it fail to get the support of the Americans and the Europeans?

One of the difficulties that faced the West was the exact size of the Soviet armed forces. Traditionally the Soviet Union had a large land-based military force. NATO agreed to withdraw only so many kilometers and the Americans could well withdraw across the ocean making us less secure. It seems what we needed was superiority in technology and a multi-national force centrally commanded. Such a strategic force would provide the tactical commanders an opportunity of maneuvering and taking whatever actions were necessary to withhold or stop aggression while other action of crisis management was taking place.

How would you describe Canada's relations with East European countries?

I think Canada's relations with Yugoslavia, Romania and Poland have always been close because these countries are trying to be more independent. Poland is leading the countries in this respect. In the history of Poland we see how uncomfortable Poland was under the Russian domination. There were times when the Poles occupied parts of Russia and now it is Russia that is occupying Poland. It is a situation based on history, culture and religion. The dominant inspiration of the Polish nationalism is the Catholic Church that opposes the military occupation of an alien imposed totalitarianism. Frequently Poland became the battlefield as armies from the East and the West invaded it. Therefore the Polish situation is the most tragic one and demands sensitivity from the West. I am not a Pole, in fact my background is Russian, but I always felt that unless Poles are allowed to live in freedom there couldn't be stability in East-West relations.

When you were Canada's ambassador to Yugoslavia did you happen to meet some of the Canadian Yugoslavs who came offered to help Tito rebuild the country?

Yes, I remember meeting quite a few of them, one being a gentleman by the name of Edel Yarasch. He was a member of the Central Committee of the Communist Party of Canada. When the rift occurred between Tito and Stalin he got into a confrontation with Tim Buck, the secretary general of the Communist Party of Canada. Yarasch felt that the rupture was an important historic event. In order to celebrate this event he gathered some two hundred or maybe more Canadians of Yugoslav extraction, chartered a ship and sailed to Yugoslavia where he and his group applauded Tito.

During the Hungarian revolution Yarasch was a great asset to me. He helped me to get Hungarians who escaped to Yugoslavia from where they than set sail to Canada and the United States. Later he became the Minister of Tourism in Yugoslavia. I introduced him to a representative of the World Bank in Europe who was able to get credits for tourism. For some time tourism brought prosperity to Yugoslavia as hotels were built, highways constructed and summer resorts opened.

There was always a debate about fascists or communists coming to Canada from Yugoslavia. What is your comment?

It was very difficult to screen undesirables and prevent them from coming to Canada. There were some who collaborated with the Nazis did come to Canada. There was a certain amount of animosity against the Yugoslav communist regime. When the foreign minister Koca Popovic came to Canada he needed RCMP protection because of a threat on his life.

Jack McCormick

The author interviewed Jack McCordick on December 8. 1984. No other diplomat served in as many Canadian posts in Eastern Europe as McCordick. He was one of the members of the first legation in the Soviet Union and was appointed ambassador for Czechoslovakia and Poland. During his time as a diplomat he took part in opening most of the Canadian legations in Eastern Europe. Besides being a diplomat abroad he was instrumental for setting up the CBC-IS which beamed messages and programs to Eastern Europe.

Compare and contrast the administration of the posts where you served?

Obviously there were differences and one can go in great length about the problems because there were considerable. And in that case in Foreign Service it was in the Soviet Union in 1943 when we (Canada) opened a mission in the middle of the war. I had been in the army and had actually been appointed as an assistant military attaché. Due to the torpedoing of our boat I was listed as missing and possibly dead. I survived and was sent to the Soviet Union because of my knowledge of the Russian language. Because the German armies besieged Moscow we were housed in the provincial city of Kubisychev. There was not much to do here. Fortunately the British mission helped us.

What was your next posting?

I was sent to Prague in March 1947 and for a short period of time I was posted to the Canadian Military Mission in Berlin. As in the case of the Soviet Union Ronald MacDonald and I opened a mission here. Then another move, back to Prague, the capital city with many more amenities than found in Moscow. It was a cultured western type of a city and not destroyed as other cities were.

The authorities here were helpful. At this time the society was quite open with western papers available. Facilities were put at our disposal and the landlord was friendly. The residence building we acquired was a splendid structure built by a French architect in a British Tudor style, the only mansion of this style for hundred miles. It had its defects like the poor electrical wiring. For six months I lived in a hotel because I could not find a suitable place. The owner wanted me to pay in US dollars. The foreign minister was Thomas Masaryk, a very western minded, gregarious, friendly character.

Were you in Prague when the Czech *coup* occurred?

Yes, I was there during it but just. I, by pure fluke or coincidence, I had been posted away to Belgrade, where we were opening another mission. I rather hoped I could deflect this decision. I wrote to Mr. Pearson saying than an officer's usefulness was limited by being bounced around too much and I had been just nine months in Berlin and eleven months in Prague, and here I was off again. But they (External Affairs) decided that had experience in opening missions and because I was a bachelor and not tied down I was chosen to go to Belgrade. The very day I set out on my trip there was public demonstrations in Prague carried out by a carefully trained and armed so-called Workers Militia, people from factories with armbands and rifles. There was a lot of maneuvering on the streets.

Within a few days the Benes government crumbled as Benes himself, a very sick man, had no choice but to allow the communist takes over. The democratic government was dismantled and replaced by a communist one. As I was driving on my way to Belgrade the radio announcer blared the alarming news about the *coup*. The Czechs and Slovaks were rather pessimistic about the outcome knowing that no country was going to intervene on their behalf. The following day I drove from Bratislava into Belgrade.

How did you feel about the *coup*?

I was disillusioned because the *coup* strikingly revealed the Soviet chicanery. The people were kidding themselves thinking that this would not happen. People were becoming more and more cynical about the Soviet intentions and practices. Personally, I was surprised by the event.

How did you find Belgrade?

I arrived in Belgrade in February and the Yugoslav-Soviet rift came in June 1949. In Belgrade we were overwhelmed with the organizational problems, considerably greater than we experienced in Prague. There were fewer facilities available than in Prague. In addition Belgrade was a more backward city with less co-operation from the authorities. At the same time the Yugoslavs were glad to see us, for our presence provided the people, in some ways, prestige and self-esteem. It seemed that the authorities were not inclined to give us help and in a way they were unable to do so. At that time Tito's regime was not too popular. We felt a certain ideological gulf between the Yugoslavs and ourselves similar to the one I experienced in Moscow.

Did the knowledge of the Russian language help you in your work in Yugoslavia?

I never learned to speak Serbian well, but I learned it well enough to deal with the people and to read the front pages of the newspapers. Serbian and Russian languages are close enough and it is surprising how much you can understand the language provided that you do not attempt to read the technical or sophisticated literature. While dealing with practical every day matters, you can do a surprising amount of work by just using two languages. I would speak very often slowly and distinctly in Russian and they (Yugoslavs) would reply in Serbian. Often we would choose another word if one had not been understood. I found quite a few people spoke German or French, which helped us in a practical way.

There is a criticism that is levied at the department of External Affairs for not having personnel who know different languages. Is it a valid criticism?

You are right although I myself would not call it a criticism. I think that is a little unfair. The whole way the External Affairs members were recruited and the sources of recruitment all combined to create a department of quality. One should remember that we were created and expanded in a short time into what is universally recognized as one of the best Foreign Service in the world. It didn't shine linguistically but it shone in practically every other way.

Did we reflect the British or the American foreign office?

It is true that the American despite the fact that Dr. Skelton and Mackenzie King were very suspicious of the British influenced us more by the British model than. We had close relationship with the British who assisted us in our missions. They helped us enormously in Moscow, Prague and Belgrade. The help was freely given and it was not meant to be repaid.

What was the nature of this assistance?

In Kubiyshev for example we lived briefly in a hotel and then we were given a building, a former malarial hospital which we used for our office. We, Lana Wilgress, Ronald MacDonald, Ronald Smith and I worked and lived there. Since we did not have cooking staff the British invited us to have meals with them in a building, which once belonged to a merchant millionaire. We insisted on paying and so finally they charged us a modest amount. There was co-operation in other ways. The British offered us the use of safe storage for our diplomatic materials.

In Belgrade the house we had for our offices was just a couple of streets away from the British embassy and since again we did not have proper way of protecting confidential material so we would stock it in suitcases, lock them up put them in the car and store in the British embassy. In the morning we would retrieve this material. All this transaction was done in a spirit of genuine co-operation.

What can you say about the instructions the legation received from the department of External Affairs?

Well here you entered the field I think I might as well speak my mind rather than dress things up. I have always been a critic of the way the instructions were given to missions and critical of the contents of these instruction. This didn't mean that there weren't significant guidelines. Sometimes Canada was interested in a particular item for example Article 2 of the United Nations Charter. Mr. Pearson would send instructions to all the missions about this article saying that this did not apply to communist countries but to those connected with NATO.

You may be sent to see some one in the Foreign Office, a minister or a lower official. Whatever was decided was in line with the Canadian foreign policy. At times the instruction was to intervene on behalf of a Canadian citizen. What the head of the post got from Ottawa would be couched in general terms. Subsequent instructions would be more detailed. At times these were too encyclopedic in their scope. For instance, the External would ask the mission to report on everything from sleeping sickness to aggression. This made things very difficult for one did not know what Ottawa wanted. I felt that we didn't get enough instructions or specific calls about our activities in our mission.

In a sense we wrote our own instructions. In other words we took the initiative and decided what could and should be done for the good of Canada. There was another way we did things. We would suggest alternatives to the solution of a problem and have Ottawa decide what was best, in their opinion, under given circumstances.

As Arnold Smith said in his interview with you that he attempted to project a certain image in the county we served. We had instructions on this too. As patriotic Canadians we felt that we were world's favorite citizens. In a joking way I would say to Ottawa that all we had to do was to say that we are Canadians and then call the police to control the crowds. It wasn't like that but we did rank very high, well above our normal specific gravity. This was artificial because certain unknown factors emerged from time to time that we did not anticipate. We did come out of the war as the third nuclear power and fourth military power.

We, indeed, had a special role. We combined Canadian realism with Canadian idealism. We recruited very highly qualified individuals for the Foreign Service. We had a government at home that was internationally minded. Yes, we were feeling our oats and with some justification. In many cases we were plowing new ground. You see in a way we were writing our own instructions. Being on the spot we could judge what was most appropriate to say and do. We could to tell Ottawa what it is like. We were happy to bring influence on certain issues which later were be approved by the United Nations.

How did the posts encourage trade?

We were told to help increase trade. That was important but we were rather slow in creating effective machinery for trade promotion. At one time

Vienna was the hub of a very substantial wheel. The commercial section covered Czechoslovakia Poland, Hungary and Yugoslavia, as well as whatever we had to do with Rumania and Bulgaria, which was almost nothing. The centralized operation of Vienna was gradually changed as commercial sections were added to the individual missions. To day (1984) I don't think Vienna covers anything other country than Austria.

One argument for the proposed closing of missions in Eastern Europe was the cost of maintaining them. Do you wish to comment?

We never know when a post may provide us with important information. Take for example, the Canadian post in Belgrade. At the beginning of the post there seemed little to do but as time went on this post became rather important source of information on Eastern Europe. We had cordial relations with the British and American embassies. The Americans alluded to the fact that something was happening between the Soviet Union and Yugoslavia. They even showed me the analysis their experts made indicating that a rift was coming. As time showed they were right. They had the piece that fitted the jigsaw puzzle. They confirmed which up to that time mere speculation was. They began sending off telegrams to Washington about this. I know that they got it right because they did something, which was very unusual and very generous, and I didn't expect it. The British often showed their documents. But now the American were eager to inform us. On one occasion the American ambassador asked me to come over and showed me the files indicating the Moscow-Belgrade rupture.

How would you grade the East European countries according to the importance Canada gave them?

I believe that the Soviet Union was the most important country. As to other countries their importance varied with the events that transpired. Yugoslav break with the Cominform was a press headline in 1949. And there was a speculation that if this could happen to one of the countries, it could happen to others. In 1956 the focus was on Hungary and in 1968 it was Czechoslovakia again. The searchlight moved where the spectacle was most interesting.

Yugoslavia was again in the spotlight on the issue of dual citizenship. What was the problem?

In 1948 a number of Canadians and Yugoslav nationalists were persuaded by Belgrade to go to Yugoslavia and help rebuild the war-torn country. After a relative short period of time some of them wanted to return to Canada. The Yugoslav government who took their passports away at their entrance to the country argued that under international law anyone who travels to the country of their origin losses the citizenship of the adopted country even though one can use the dual citizenship stance in other countries. This issue became bitter but in the end the Canadian lawyers agreed that the Yugoslav government had a legal argument.

Canada took the position that the emigrants had been lured in bad faith, and been given promises which were not kept. They did not get their passports back until many years later. I felt that this was a very unpleasant way of operating and could create bad relations between the two countries. As a result of this incidence the Canadian passport office made a significant alteration by inserting a clause in the passport, which said, "this passport is the property of the Canadian government." Following these episode relations improved between Canada and Yugoslavia. However, the label "communist" continued to be used even though Yugoslavia broke with the Soviet Union.

Detention of Polish Art Treasures was a "sore spot" in Canadian Polish relations. Would you comment on this?

I don't think there was any officer in the External Affairs who did not have to do some work on the problem of the detention of Polish Art Treasures. It was a huge problem and it is very hard to summarize. But eventually positions crystallized and were simplified a bit. The Polish position remained the same. These treasures were part of the Polish heritage. They meant much to them in a way similar to Hungarians' claim for the crown of St. Stephen. Every country has a collection of symbols and for the Poles the Treasures were the symbols of what Poland stood for.

Early after the War Canada accepted the Polish argument about the ownership of these national relics and wanted desperately to return them to Poland. The Canadian experts were also concerned about the deterioration of the collection. To the Polish and Canadian experts' special care was urgently needed to preserve the precious items. However, there was another problem. Some individuals and groups wanted the collection to be returned to Poland immediately while other groups were not too certain if such a move would ensure the safety of these national treasures should they be returned to Poland. One such group was the Quebec provincial government which under Premier Maurice Duplessis with the aid of some of the Polish émigrés did not wish them to return to Poland for fear that they would not receive proper care or be whisked away to Russia.

Could you say that Poland was considered to be a special country and the Poles were just different from other Slavic people?

Yes, indeed Poland was a special nation. No matter what the government they choose or what was imposed on them they were different. They react in a different way. Sometimes it is predictable for they react in a strong manner. As one writer said the Poles "get up on the horse and charge despite consequences." It is the enormous strength of Polish nationalism that makes them ready for any combat. The Czechs look for a quiet way out like a reed in the wind. The Czechs are cautious and ready for compromise or just bear things stoically.

I think Polish nationalism nurtured for centuries by tradition, history and the Catholic religion developed certain characteristics. Polishness is seen in every thing the Poles say and do. Polishness I came to admire when I lived in Poland. Poland is extremely Polish. It is impregnated with "polishness" that is the way they do things. They are generous and nice people to live with. They display the old fashion courtesy. I have lived and worked in the Soviet Union, Poland, Czechoslovakia and Yugoslavia and have traveled in Hungary, Bulgaria and Rumania. All these countries are different from one another. I think Poland stands out as the most different of all the Slavic countries.

The Poles speak their own mind even when they do it at their own risk. When you go to a restaurant in Prague people speak in whispers but in Poland they speak and sing in loud voices and even make critical remarks about the regime.

I understand that Polish government officials are also different from officials in other East European countries.

I am tempted to say that they are more civilized. They are certainly more polished. They never speak in slogans. When a Soviet official speaks he uses slogans as part of his vocabulary. I never heard that in Poland. Also socially they are very available, more so than officials in other countries. You can invite Polish officials, deputy ministers and their wives and they are happy to come. And you can mix old regime with a new one and every thing goes well. On one occasion we were at the Belgian embassy for dinner at which time there was a young prince who was married to a Belgian. There was also a vice minister of peasant origin who was perfectly at home with the prince and me.

I understand you were also in Hungary. What were your impression of the people and the government of Hungary?

I have visited Hungary many times, once when I was eighteen years of age. In 1964 just after I finished my term as an ambassador to Czechoslovakia I was instructed by the department of External Affairs to go to Budapest and open official discussions with Hungarian authorities in view of exchanging diplomatic missions. I was received with utmost courtesy and hospitality. One issue that came up was dual nationality.

Were Canadian-East European relations carried on in the context of East-West relations?

Well there are always bilateral aspects and often we wanted to develop them, for example trade. But I think in general they were in the framework of East-West relations. I am a strong supporter of NATO and certainly that is what Ottawa wanted. We did naturally have purely Canadian problems that we had to work out ourselves.

How can we be sure that immigrants from Eastern Europe will be loyal Canadian citizens?

I think that anybody wanting to leave these countries was almost by definition an opponent of the system and no one need to worry. At another level, a more serious level, Canadian democratic realism being what it is we would know that communist regimes do indulge in skull drudgery even though Canada is not a threat to anyone. However there are always some immigrants who were spies.

Since you were involved in CBC-IS as the department of External Affairs' representative and its policy adviser, would you like to outline your experiences in this capacity?

I was the first person to maintain that the department of External Affairs had the right to guide the CBC-IS (CBS International Service) which was rather a free wheeling institution lacking a uniform mandate and a system of operation. It did not speak on the behalf of Canada but was rather a mouthpiece for such ethnic groups as Ukrainians, Poles and Czechs. Some Canadians questioned the loyalty of these groups.

Thereupon the department of External Affairs was asked to monitor the CBC-IS and to lay ground rules for its operation. I was chosen as the liaison officer for this task. I used to commute from Ottawa to Montreal, the seat of the CBC-IS operation, advising the personnel. At the beginning I just investigated and observed the operation. I became more aware of what the speakers said some of which was contrary to Canada's foreign policy.

There were two objectives that the Canada wished to achieve by the CBC-IS; first and foremost to truthfully portray the image of Canada to Eastern Europe and secondly to engage in a psychological warfare against the communist regimes. United States and Great Britain put tremendous pressured on Canada and considered Canada's contribution, though relatively small, was nevertheless important. I did a lot of surveying and analyzing to discern how effective CBC-IS was. I was very, very doubtful. Because our two friends, United States and Great Britain, wanted us to remain in the "club" and so we did. I realized that it was in the interest of Canada that this service should continue for although we were a minor member we were at times asked for our opinions. In the context of the times I still think that we did the right thing although I was unconvinced of its effectiveness.

Did you meet anyone who listened to the CBC-IS broadcasts?

One can talk a long time about the sort of people who listened to the broadcasts. Are these convinced democrats or are the people who like playing with a short-wave set. Would these listeners help to undermine the communist regime when and if the war broke out?

Would you again outline the objectives of the CBC-IS?

We wanted to project Canada. For example, when we spoke in Czech we spoke of Canada using the knowledge we had of Czechoslovakia. By and large the Czech émigrés did a reasonable job talking about Canada as their adopted country. Some of them wanted to wage psychological war against the Czech communist government. To make sure of the content of their presentation I examined their scripts before they spoke over the radio.

In your opinion how did the Voice of America differ from the BBC broadcasts?

I am not sure about that. I think that the foreign office always had a kind of control that we are seeking to banish. The Voice of America was really George Keenan who later became the American ambassador to Moscow. I can't remember how the State Department did it. I know that it was not freewheeling although individuals were given freedom to exercise their talents but under supervision.

How did East European governments react to the CBC-IS?

They did not like the broadcast because for them these broadcasts were just another sign of western interference. I do not know whether Canada received any official complaints. Neither do I know whether we complained about the Soviet broadcasts.

Once in Warsaw on the National Day reception I had a conversation with a senior member of the Polish Communist Party. One generally does not meet such people and so I took advantage of the occasion. I said that I read in the Polish paper that the Polish government labeled Canada as a member of NATO and an imperialist country. It was mentioned in the paper eighteen times. I pointed out that this was an error for we are no longer a colony of Great Britain. We are independent as we went from colony to a sovereign nation. And I do not know how by any stretch of linguistic imagination you could label Canada as "imperialist." In defending my country I should object to being grouped with common imperialist countries in the eyes of Poland. Anyway this label is dated for empires are all gone. O yes, the Japanese still call their man emperor and the Shaw of Iran is a type of an emperor. Virtually there are no emperors but there still exists one big empire. It has closely controlled colonies. You know the name of this empire. And I really had him. Anyway, I said to him, perhaps I should make a formal complaint to the Polish Foreign Office. Or would you prefer to see to it that another article is written in which you clarify the term "imperialist". Of course, I knew that nothing would be done but I had fun—it made my day.

How important is it for Canada to maintain relations with Eastern Europe?

Well, that's hard question to answer. I think in my view it is important to maintain missions abroad. They are important in furthering trade and cultural exchanges. In Canada we have many Canadians of foreign extraction that require assistance to communicate with their relatives in Europe. If we do not do this then who is going to do it? I do not think that we exert enough influence for good or peace. I don't think that we that we have been successful in converting other people towards our way of thinking. We often think that we have a missionary goal; I don't think so.

Do you think we ever had such a mission and were we successful?

I don't think so. I think we're always preaching to the converted. There are two kinds of converts, those who believe in the West and those who do not need conversion. And then there are those who are convinced that they are right as Marxists and no preaching is going to change them. There is the question of international practice should we be the odd man out.

But there is another question that is begging for an answer. The question is whether the people of Eastern Europe will ever see a change in the Soviet bloc countries. How can we, Canadians, encourage these people to be patient and hopeful? Seeing Canadian flag on our car and observing Canadian art exhibits does give these people courage to "hold on." There are better days to come. Missions also have Canadian point of view expressed in the press by their own writers using sources filtered through a mesh of Canadian interests, knowledge and background. We should not be ignorant of anything that is happening in the world. We could make very good use of retired ambassadors who once served in Eastern Europe and could provide a variety of views from which a consensus can be formed.

Does Eastern Europe provide us with means of understanding the Soviet Union?

There is much criticism of Czechoslovakia and East Germany who reportedly have increased the number of Soviet missiles on their territory. That means that if it is strong enough to come to the surface then it is very strong. Because of this exerted pressure people are reluctant to speak in public. You cannot start a campaign to encourage public demonstrations in Czechoslovakia; it wouldn't work. And it would get us into a useless and cumbersome situation. But at the same time we are able our proposals for such objectives as armed reduction without appearing to be arrogant and all wise. We are not operating in a total vacuum, for we are not only facing generals in the Kremlin but also public opinion. And therefore our presence in the country along with the short-wave broadcasting can be useful and effective. The Poles and the Czechs know a great deal about what is going on in the outside world.

Is communism the same in all the East European countries?

Something I have given much thought which, on the one hand impresses me and on the other hand, depresses me. The Soviet regime has been in the saddle for a long time having total control of public opinion, punishing the dissidents, preventing their citizens to travel abroad and forbidding contacts with foreigners. As far as contacts are concerned the Soviet Empire could be on the moon. And with constant propaganda and ideological preaching Soviet Union has introduced a new vocabulary.

What is white in one country is black in another. A good example is the word democracy. It is used everyday both in the West and in the East with a total different meaning. Words like freedom, honor, lying and immigration have a different meaning in the Soviet Union and its satellites than in North America and Europe.

But there is something that is positive, for in Poland, Czechoslovakia and Hungary these terms have retained their true meaning among many of the people of these countries. When we use our own Western definitions of these words the people in the Soviet bloc countries know what we are talking about. In a way the Russians have lost contact with the rest of the world and have invented their own vocabulary. On the other hand I am amazed when I talk with the young Poles. They know a lot about the West.

To what extent are foreigners watched and followed in Eastern Europe?

In my experience I do not remember that I was followed in Eastern Europe but in Moscow I was. The military personnel were followed. They were followed closely and at times the Canadian government expressed its objections to such tactics. Yes, we were watched and our conversations scrutinized. It was routine to have microphones in our rooms and in other vulnerable places. I suspect that following Western citizens is a routine assignment.

I was never doing anything that was wrong. I was never a ploy to go out and spy or take photographs of airfields. And the way security is organized your opportunities for spying was limited. If you plan to go on a tour to see something in Poland like a battlefield or castle the Polish security plot your movement. They know where you are at all times. In most towns you pass at the intersection with police standing there. All our cars have diplomatic license plates that identify the embassy of the country. Policeman usually takes out his notebook and makes a note pretending that he does not know the country to which you belong. So at the end of the day he may have three or four identifications. Mr. McCordick left Warsaw at a certain time, turned south and traveled on a certain highway. When you register at the hotel for the night there is another identification they plot you around. They also know that not all of us are spies. We do not go out and meet an agent in a graveyard.

What are some of the ways the post gets information?

Reading the press is one of the ways. There is whole art of reading the press in communist countries, not just daily papers but also trade journals even literary journals. It is a combination of art and science. The findings are surprisingly revealing particularly by the way they say things. The selection of what news should be included in the paper gives a message. By reading and analyzing the press critically you recognize the missing links and you learn where you can find these links.

What about contacts with the people?

In Poland contacts with ordinary people was not difficult to arrange but in the Soviet Union it was extremely difficult. Most of the contacts would be incidental. I would consider it most unfair to place the people in certain political category by my questions. I tried not to place any of the citizens in trouble by my questions.

What do you think of cultural exchanges?

I react to the exchange in the same way as I react to short-wave broadcasting. I know that a lot of the exchanges originate in Canada and France and people appreciate performing arts, but I do not know how much it means to better relations. It is enjoyable and people rush to get tickets but what does prove?

I wish to relate a personal contact that began well but became controversial. Hungarians in Warsaw built a new commercial section in the basement of which was a type of an inn. The Hungarian ambassador whom I knew quite well invited me to an inauguration party since I could spoke Russian. Beside myself there were also the French ambassador and his wife, a Swede and a Russian and his wife. Along with these guests there was a Polish couple, and an artist who worked for the government. She was sitting besides the Soviet ambassador's wife. During the conversation the artist addressed me using my first name. Next time we met he artist told me that the Soviet ambassador's wife said to her "didn't you know that he is NATO."

Jack Pickersgill

The author interviewed Jack Pickersgill on May 23, 1984. For years he was the personal secretary of prime minister Mackenzie King. He was persuaded to enter politics and the Cabinet of St. Laurent as a minister of Immigration. During his tenure the Hungarian Revolution, 1956, occurred. Thousands of Hungarians left their native country and migrated elsewhere including Canada. Some 37,000 of these refugees entered Canada. More than any other Canadian Pickersgill was responsible for this massive influx of educated and skilled Hungarians.

Could you give me some of the details leading to Canada's involvement in the Hungarian Revolution?

The Hungarian Revolution occurred about the same time as the Suez Crisis; in fact this crisis prevented the allies from dealing effectively with the Revolution. Prime Minister St. Laurent was irritated by this coincidence for he felt the allies could have restrained the Soviet Union. I felt that the allies did mitigate the pain created by the revolution by accepting refugees. I argued that if we did not help these unfortunate refugees they might be forced to return to Hungary where they would probably face some type of punishment.

Whereas other countries did not want to accept students Canada did. I got exceptionally busy persuading Canadian university authorities to welcome Hungarian students into their institutions. Most of the universities responded positively to my urgings. For instance, I received help from Sydney Smith, the president of the University of Toronto, and I made arrangements for the whole forestry department to move from Hungary to the University of British Columbia. I found places for some 10,000 refugees crowded in Austria, Holland and England where they stayed to until April and May when the weather in Canada was more moderate.

What about security clearance and medical examination?

These refugees were medically examined until they arrived in Canada. I met some opposition from one or two of my colleagues who argued that without a thorough screening one did not know what type of people were entering our country. Some may be carrying serious diseases. In fact the refugees were not landed immigrants until they were examined and accepted.

The ones who did not pass the medical examination were admitted as visitors and were given appropriate treatment for their ailments.

How many were there who were considered "undesirable"?

Perhaps 500 out of 35,000, some of them wanted to return to Hungary. Anyone who wished to go back home the Canadian government made it easier for him or her to do so. I do now know of anyone who remained in Canada was found to be subversive. Even though many of the refugees were well educated and skilled, they found it difficult to adjust to the language and the customs of the new country.

Fortunately in the early part of 1957 the new-comers, many of them students, found jobs, but in later months they found it difficult to get employment. One of the good features of the situation was that many were single and young enough to adjust to the new environment.

When you look back is there anything different you would have done with respect to the refugees?

Yes, I thought that it was a disgrace to the Western World to continue having refugee camps operating many years after the war was over. I tried some eight years later to get other desirable individuals to immigrate to Canada particularly those who had relatives here. This was particularly true with Polish immigrants who had relatives in Canada. To screen these people we took into consideration families that applied to come to Canada and the recommendations of the Canadian-Polish Congress and the Canadian-Jewish Congress.

As you look back do you note significant changes in our policy towards Eastern Europe?

Well of course there were profound diplomatic changes since the Czech *coup*. King who knew Masaryk personally was shaken by the events. He was also concerned about the possible involvement of Canada in European affairs. But St. Laurent and Pearson felt that Canada must show her solidarity with the Allies.

Would you say that Canada follows the United States in her foreign policy?

There is that perception and does have some bases in fact. Ninety percent of our foreign transaction is with the United States. When we were talking about recognizing Communist China before the United States we felt that it would be an insult to our close neighbour if we did recognize it. And after all, the recognition would be of marginal benefit to us but a major insult to the Americans.

We should remember that we do not automatically do what the Americans want. For instance the American wanted us to break all relations with Cuba, but we refused to do so. When I was the minister of Transport the Russians wanted permission to fly from Gander to Havana or from Montreal to Havana. I knew that this would be offensive to the Americans so I said that we could reach an to agreement whereby we would allow you to fly over Siberia to Japan provided that you allow us to fly over Siberia en route to Japan. I did not get another request of this nature again. This was dropped.

Was there ever a political reason to help East European that is did Canada help immigrants in order to have them vote for the party that helped them?

No I don't think so. Certainly this did not enter my mind. We helped people because they were in need. I agree that at the same time as politicians we appreciated their vote. When you consider that one third of the Canadian population is neither French nor English and many belong to the East European group it is only natural that all political parties were interested in their vote.

Generally speaking the government resisted of being drawn into ethnic agenda particularly in "liberation" of such countries as Ukraine. We had in one sense greater sympathy for such ethnic groups as Poles and Czechoslovaks because of their past struggle for independence. Personally I visited most of the East European countries except Romania and Bulgaria.

In what way was Canadian government's policy towards communism and the Soviet Union different that of the United States?

There seemed to have been great fear of communism in the United States. Unlike Canada the United States was very cautious with whom it carried on cultural exchanges and even trade. They did not like us selling wheat to the Russians. Every government since the war had been more or less paranoid about the Soviet Union, but I don't think that we were. Yes, we regarded the Russians as a potential threat, but very few Canadians believed that the Soviet Union was more imperialistic than the United States.

Prime Minister Mackenzie King was troubled by the Gouzenko's revelations. He also understood that there were large communist parties in France and Italy that gave some an impression that soon communism would spread to all the countries of Europe. The fear factor contributed to the creation of the NATO. It is doubtful whether the Russians ever contemplated the conquest of Europe.

Benjamin Rogers

Benjamin Rogers was interviewed by the author on May 31, 1984. Rogers served in the very difficult time of the Cold War as a charge d'affaires in Czechoslovakia from 1950-1952. After his assignment in Canada was completed he was sent to Peru.

What are your recollections of the conditions in Czechoslovakia during your time as the Canadian charge d'affaires?

I arrived in Prague in 1950 and I was there two years. The communists were firmly entrenched when I arrived. It was a very uncomfortable situation living behind the Iron Curtain at that time. We always felt that we had to do everything well and carefully so as not to invite retaliation from the government. So we were living under certain tension. I remember in the fall of 1950 I was having trouble with my eyes and so I went to an eye specialist in Prague. He examined my eyes and said "You're under a quite a strain here, aren't you" and I said "yes." He then said there is nothing wrong with your eyes, what you need is a holiday. Actually, we were going off to ski in Austria in two weeks time and I did not have to change my glasses.

Did the Czech government harass you or your legation staff?

Yes, there was harassment in the sense that the authorities questioned some of our staff in order to get confidential information. I remember one time a house servant said to my wife, "Do you know that we have to report to the police every time we speak to you or any one from the foreign country?" "I have to tell you that after the party at the Canadian legation the police asked me whether there were any Czechs there and did Mr. Rogers take aside any of the guests and spoke to them.?" Police cars frequently followed us.

The police closely watched the members of the government and the civil servants. We would invite diplomats to a reception but they would not come. Oh yes on our National Day we would get a token representation when a few would appear.

On one occasion we received an application for an exit VISA for a young Czech Officer of the Foreign Ministry who was posted to Ottawa so we planned a party for him. So I met him and said that my wife and I would like to have a little reception for you where you could meet some of our diplomatic staff. He hesitated a bit and so I said maybe I could speak to your superiors. The superior officer replied that he would have to consult his wife. The young officer's wife did not come for she was away at that time. The appearance of the officer at the party was an unusual concession, for the members of the ministry did not come to our dinner parties.

Poles were different. The Polish ambassador was an engaging type of a fellow. I think that he was a journalist and spoke excellent English. I remember that he turned up at the American embassy and not seeing any one from the Soviet bloc countries inquired whether they were invited. The answer was yes.

Would you mind relating some incidents that portray the difficulties encountered by your mission and other individuals?

The people from India had created wider relations with the Czechs than we did. On one occasion I met an Indian export/import corporation lawyer who was forbidden to practice law even though he knew the Czech language well. He came to my office to speak to me. The Czech authorities had the conversation recorded as the office was bugged. This Indian lost his export-import license and he was forced to find work in a factory labouring with professor and former Czech attaché to Canada.

Was there any value in having a Canadian legation in Czechoslovakia?

I think that our presence heartened the people in Czechoslovakia who still hoped that there would be a change and that somebody would come in and rescue them. There was a lot of rather unrealistic thinking on the part of the Czechs. They thought that somehow or other the situation would change for the better would have democracy in their country restored.

I remember that on the first May Day parade I attended there was obviously great enthusiasm, for the people felt that they were on the winning side. Since that time the people have lost some of the enthusiasm. There was also evidence that some of the communists were becoming disillusioned. Of some importance some of these communists were long-time members of the Party. They were beginning to realize that the communist system was not good.

There seems to be some cracks in the Kremlin wall.

I made friends with rather interesting Yugoslav diplomat who oddly enough did not feel comfortable in neither the Western nor the Soviet group. Although a communist he was harassed by the Czechs.

I know that it is difficult to rank Canada's preferences as to East European countries. How would you rate them?

I suppose the fact that we had missions established in Poland, Yugoslavia, and Czechoslovakia early after the war these countries would be rated more important that some of the others. We had some trade with these countries and we were discussing the solution of claims for Canadians whose properties were seized by the government.

Did you have any personal contact with the people?

There was common knowledge that there was certain amount of tension between the two groups but again we did not have enough contact to verify this assumption. I remember driving back from Vienna something went wrong with the car; it was stuck in the second gear. I stopped at a garage man who knew some English and had it fixed the vehicle. I hoped that he did not get in trouble for talking to a foreigner.

Did you meet anyone who later defected to the West?

When I just arrived at the legation I received a postcard posted in Munich from a doctor who medically examined prospective immigrants to Canada. Several years later I ran into this doctor on the north shore of Prince Edward Island. It was quite by accident. We were having dinner one night with friends and one of them said we were talking to some Czechs who are camping about a hundred yards from here. Would you like to meet them?

It turned out that it was that same doctor who processed immigrants wishing to come to Canada. He told me that he had gone with his wife and two children to visit a friend and to do some mushroom picking. Czechs are crazy about mushrooms. They wandered further and further into the forest. All of a suddenly they found an American cigarette package. Now they realized that they crossed the border. Their inclination was to go back. His wife said no way are we going back. They were picked up and taken to a refugee camp and two years later they immigrated to Canada.

Ben Seaborn

The author interviewed Seaborn on May 29, 1984.He was with the East European division of the department of External Affairs during the years 1956-57 and became the head of this division for the years 1962 to 1964. He served in the Canadian embassy in Moscow from 1959 to 1962 and for a year and half he served as an observer in Vietnam. Upon return to Canada he was made the head of East European division in 1966.

Can you summarize your experiences in your dealing with Eastern Europe?

During my years of service relating to Eastern Europe the relationship with the Soviet Union and her satellites were strained. I was fascinated with Khrushchev for he was a man full of energy and exuberance. This rather uncontrolled exuberance got him into trouble during the Cuban missile crisis. At the same time he provided a breath of fresh air following the death of Stalin. As I found out later, Khrushchev was also a dictator.

On what were your reports to Ottawa based?

I received information through contacts with personnel of other embassies, the Soviet ministry of Foreign Affairs and through newspapers and periodicals. Although I did not speak Russian I nevertheless had contacts with the Cultural Ministry, Foreign Ministry and Ministry of Foreign trade. From 1958 there was a drive on the part of the Soviet Union to initiate such exchanges as forestry, mining and cultural. Through bilateral agreements Montreal Symphony Orchestra and Maureen Forester performed in Russia.

Could you make some comments on other aspects of activities Canada had with the Soviet Union.

Yes, there were some commercial opportunities particularly in the sale of grain due to a failure of Russian crops. We wanted to initiate scientific exchanges related to the north. They made a lot of noises about their intention to develop this region but when the Canadian scientists from the National

Research Council of Canada arrived in the Soviet Union they were terribly disappointed. Oh, yes they were wined and dined in Leningrad but never got to the northern part of Russia. It took a very long time for the Russians to trust us. In many cases permission to visit certain parts of Russia would be given but with many restrictions as to when you could visit.

Talking about restrictions, what was life like at the Canadian Embassy in Moscow?

Well, as a pampered diplomat it wasn't bad at all. You ate perfectly well because most of the food was imported and you lived in infinitely better quarters than the Russians ever hoped to live, except for those of the very top levels. We had to keep reminding ourselves that we were constantly under surveillance. But we went on the assumption that most of our conversations were probably bugged. We had militiamen stationed at the gate to protect us and also to keep an eye on us. There were a number of unpleasant incidents whereby a Russian who came to the Canadian Embassy to inquire about a trip to Canada would be roughed up by the guards.

How was travel in Russia?

I managed to do a fair amount of traveling with the usual frustrations. You think you are all set to go and at the last moment they say, "I am sorry for there is no hotel room for you or all the trains are full." Not withstanding these irritants I did get a certain amount of travel in. We were carefully watched when we were outside of Moscow, but by and large we were left alone during which time we had some opportunities for human contacts. And even with the limited amount of spoken Russian I was able to have some conversations on the train or in the restaurant Russians were curious about foreigners who to them wore strange clothing and spoke a different language they were accustomed to hear.

We never traveled alone; either we traveled with another member of the Canadian embassy or with someone from another embassy. Because our staff was small our embassy could not afford to have another member to be away at the same time. I thoroughly enjoyed my stay in Moscow first under the ambassador David Johnson and later under Arnold Smith. Fortunately my wife and my two children also enjoyed it. It was during the time of great changes in the Soviet Union. Our children attended an Anglo-American school where they got along quite well. Of course they were frustrated by their inability to consort with the Russian children. The congenial diplomatic community especially the Western one more than compensated these frustrations. Most of the personnel in the diplomatic community were of high quality. But when I first arrived in Moscow from Paris I faced a cultural shock, for the enormous differences between the two cities.

John Holmes described to me some of the incidents, which were not pleasant while he was in Moscow. "They would invite us to socials and then insult us."

We had wonderful civilized parties when we were there. I remember my wife having great fun dancing with an old guy as he whirled her on the floor. I did not experience the unfortunate experience Holmes had while he was in Moscow. Of course, he was in the Soviet Union at the height of the Cold War when all Westerners were considered enemies of the Kremlin. With the arrival of"relaxation" under Khrushchev there was an honest attempt at "peaceful co-existence."

I understand that you and your colleague, Max Wershop, negotiated agreements with Hungary, Bulgaria and Romania. What was the nature of these negotiations?

In the early 1960's Canada was anxious to establish diplomatic relations with these three countries. Canada had relations with Poland, Czechoslovakia and Yugoslavia since the middle of World War II. Using his legal and diplomatic skills Wershop was able to find solutions to the issue of international claims negotiate some trade and work on the problem of reunification of families. Although we recognized these countries diplomatically we did not establish resident diplomats until later.

Arnold Smith

Arnold Smith, who the author interviewed on June 6, 1984, was a career diplomat attached to the British legation in 1940. Three years later he was assigned to Moscow where L. D. Wilgress was the minister. Master of a number of foreign languages and possessing an eagerness to learn the customs of the countries to which he was assigned Smith became a specialist of Canadian and Soviet foreign policies. He was appointed Canadian ambassador to the Soviet Union in 1961.

How would you characterize the Russians?

I liked the Russians enormously; they were very creative people but politically they were backward. Although clever, Stalin made serious mistakes. He installed puppets in East European countries and instead of co-operating with them he dominated them. I was shocked to hear that the Russians wanted to occupy Istanbul. Stalin was quite capable conquering the whole world, but his motive was predominantly defensive. I think Stalin did not want communism in countries he could not control. To understand them one needs to go back into their history. They were occupied by the Swedes, Turks and Germans and therefore adopted a policy of defence.

What was Canada's view of Eastern Europe?

Canada felt that peace in Europe was of vital importance to Canada. For this reason Canadians contributed manpower and war materiel in the Second World War. I think we played a big part in influencing Americans. Some of them wanted to build a wall around North America and have nothing to do with the world events. We argued for a world body through which collective wisdom could be shared. Some political observers claim that Canadian policies were shaped by the United States. On the contrary, many aspects of NATO, particularly Article II was suggested by Canada. Escott Reid was one of diplomats who helped drawing up the constitution of this world organization. The Americans and ourselves do not consider us small and unimportant except. For instance, we decided not to be involved in the Suez Crisis before the Americans made up their minds.

What was Trudeau's opinion of Foreign Service?

I do not think he really understood the purpose of diplomatic service; he thought it was just political reporting. On one occasion he said he could easily get better reports from the New York Times. It wasn't what I had to say to him in my report, but how effective I was in influencing him and his government. Of equal importance it was to estimate how influential I, as a member of the Foreign Service can be in my contacts with other countries. To claim that Foreign Service is merely a matter of management is utterly madness. Ambassador's influence is based on his ability to influence others.

I understand that you and L.D. Wilgress had different opinions about the Soviet Union's aggressive foreign policy in the early post World War II years.

Yes for I felt that the only way the Soviet Union could be controlled was by a "containment policy." Many political analysts argued that in all parts of the world whether it is Europe, Southeast Asia, Africa or Latin America Soviet Union had to be kept at bay. The formation of NATO, NORAD and SEATO were alliances to address the aggressive policies of Moscow. This "containment policy" was the creation of George Keenan, a member of the American State department and at onetime the American ambassador to the United States.

I was very fond of Keenan and met him from time to time. Later in life I changed my assessment of the Soviet Union. In my opinion Russia was very conscious of the enormous sacrifice she paid in the Second World War in terms of men and materiel. She did not want this carnage to ever happen again and consequently she began to build "military" walls around herself and form alliances. The subjection of Eastern Europe by means of communist parties and secret police was aimed to achieve this end.

Hamilton Southam

I interviewed H. Southam on June 5, 1984. He worked in the Canadian legation in Stockham from 1948 to 1953; from 1953 to 1859 he was stationed in Ottawa. Then in 1959 he was made charge affaires in Warsaw and from 1960 to 1963 he served as Canadian ambassador.

Your appointment to Poland as an ambassador coincided with the return of the Polish Art Treasures to Poland.

Yes, the solution to the problem of the Treasures began sometime before I arrived in Warsaw in March 1959. I knew in December 1958 that I would be going to Warsaw. While I was in Ottawa getting ready for my new assignment a Polish delegation headed by Dr. Jerzy Szyblowski a Bohdan Marconi, arrived to arrange the transfer of the deposit in the Bank of Montreal to the Polish legation. The greater portion of the Treasures was in the Quebec Provincial Museum, Quebec City. Those in the Bank of Montreal were the crowning sword, Guttenberg Bible, Chopin's manuscripts and crown jewels.

Anyway, four charming Poles arrived in Ottawa before Christmas and spent Christmas there. They came to my house for lunch one day accompanied by the third secretary of the Polish embassy. I remember how amusing they were as each one took the opportunity to speak to me privately, earshot away from my guests, assuring me that they were not communists but were only interested in the return of the Polish Treasures. And they did this with so much charm and grace. Later when I went to Poland I kept seeing these four gentlemen often.

What was it like in Poland at the time of your arrival?

Well, Gomulka was in power in 1956 and the atmosphere was a bit freer. I was able to invite Poles to the house and to the embassy. People were free to invite me to their houses or flats reminding one of the types of accommodations I found in Western Europe. I remember Jack McCordick who was our ambassador in Prague coming to stay with us and we gave him and other quests one of our usual dinners. He couldn't believe how free we were. His experience in Prague was just the opposite. Later on he became Canadian ambassador to Poland.

Were Canada's relations with Poland considered special?

Well, they were special for me because I was there. Yes, as I reflect, they were special. I am not certain whether others in the Canadian government would share the same view. There were, in my opinion, a number of reasons for these special relations. The Polish ethnic community in Canada was much larger than the Yugoslav, Romanian, Czechoslovakian or Bulgarian ethnic communities. Secondly, the Polish community represented a wider spectrum of the population as it not only included intellectuals but also peasants who came to Canada prior and after World War I. Thirdly, Poles and Canadians fought together against the Germans in the Second World War in Italy, in Normandy, in the air and on the sea.

There was also the fact the Catholic nature of Poland appealed to the Canadian Catholics. When I was appointed charges d'affaires to Poland, Norman Robertson remarked that I would really like Poland. And so I did.

Canada was interested in increasing trade and widening her contacts with Poland. Would you mind commenting on this statement?

All Canadian legations addressed this item of trade. I was not able to do very much in that respect. Although we did not have a commercial officer in our embassy, the Canadian trade counselor stationed in Copenhagen dropped in two three times a year and stayed at the legation for several days. We also had visits from the representative of the Canada Wheat Board. I know that trade with Poland increased immensely in the 1970's and 1980's. We thought that we would get a contract for the electrification of Poland. The Americans got it.

You put your finger on an area I am vitally interested, namely cultural and academic exchanges. I believe that we can exert our influence by exchanges rather than by military and political means. I discovered that the Polish people on every level were eager to develop contacts with Canadians. Intellectuals, scientists, writers, musicians and artists were anxious to have meaningful exchanges. I was able to put to put some of the Polish artists in contact with Canadian ones. When I returned to Canada I helped to develop cultural relations branch of the External Affairs.

Did you meet anyone who listened to CBC-IS?

No not really and in any case the reception was not that good. At home we had a wave band radio but seldom was anyone able to get good reception. Perhaps it was better in the countryside than in the city. In any case it did interest Poles who had relatives in Canada. Certainly it was low key and if it wasn't I would have heard about it officially. It did a good job in linking Canadians and Poles together.

When you were in Poland were there many requests for the Poles wishing to come to Canada?

Yes, family re-unification was an important element in our immigration policy. We had a large immigration section and a busy one at that. There were many Polish families in Canada who wanted to be united with families in Poland by immigrating to Canada.

Was the Canadian government concerned with security even though most of the Poles were anti-communist?

Every Canadian Visa section in the world had an official responsible for security. In the best of circumstances security problems do occur.

What in your opinion was the reason for the rise and the success of the Solidarity movement?

Well, obviously the Solidarity movement was an expression of Polish hope for more freedom and independence. I remember at the time of the Solidarity days I was very concerned about this hope for I realized that no change could come about in Poland unless there was a fundamental change in the Soviet Union. I was afraid that the Solidarity would go too far. It began sending messages to other labour organizations in socialist countries. I wasn't surprised when General Jaruszelski appeared on the scene and cracked down. When I was asked to comment on this event I said to the consternation of some that this was inevitable. I said that I hope that Jaruszelski would do what was to be done with delicacy so as not to give the Russians motive to invade Poland.

As far as you can gather what was the reaction of Canadian public opinion to the imposition of the martial law on Poland?

The Canadian public reaction was an outrage a feeling that I shared tempered by a feeling of helplessness. We as Canadians went to war in 1939 when Nazi Germany invaded Poland and here in 1981 we were helpless. There was nothing the Canadian government could do. We could only hope that significant changes would occur in the Soviet Union. But I did not see this happening in the next twenty to twenty-five years.

In the absence of an official opposition to the Polish regime the Roman Catholic Church has played this role. Could you comment on this statement?

Well, of course when I was in Poland the Catholic Church was, apart from the Party, the real force with which to be reckoned. There was no doubt that the Church occupied the first place in the minds of the people. But the Church found itself in the same situation as the Solidarity, politically helpless. Yes, the Church could bare witness about the real truth about Poland and cement the loyalty of the vast majority of the Poles, as did the Solidarity.

Our little girl turned seven when we were in Poland. She told us that she would like to go to the Polish school rather than the little school attached to the French embassy. We said certainly and so one day in September she disappeared down the street with her two Polish friends into the school. She spent three years in the Polish school system.

I remember the first winter our daughter was in school the government decreed that all crucifixes had to be removed from the classrooms. In addition the government forbade the teaching of catechism in public schools. But the Polish people found a solution; they taught religion in the church after class hours. My daughter has retained the Polish language and uses it when speaking to her friends, who with their parents, immigrated to Canada.

BIBLIOGRAPHY

Primary Sources

Manuscript Documents

Department of External Affairs, RG 19, 20, 25

Memoranda to the Cabinet

Interviews of the Canadian Diplomats

Permanent Court of International Justice Series

Printed Sources

Canadian Annual Reports, Ottawa

Canadian Annual Review of Politics and Public Affairs

Debates. *House of Commons*, Ottawa

Secondary Sources

Books

The American Educator Encyclopedia, The United Educators Incorporated Publishers, NY, 1947.

Balawyder Aloysius, *Canadian-Soviet Relations Between the Wars*, University of Toronto Press, 1972.

----*The Odyssey of the Polish Treasures*, St. Francis Xavier University Press, 1978.

----*The Maple Leaf and the White Eagle, Canadian-Polish Relations, 1945-1962,* Columbia University Press, 1981.

----*Canadian-Soviet Relations, 1939-1962,* (ed.) Mosaic Press, Toronto, 1981.

----*In the Clutches of the Kremlin, Canadian-East European Relations, 1945-1962,* Colombia University Press, 2000.

Bromke, Adam, *Poland, The Last Decade,* Mosaic Press, Oakville, 1981.

Birnbaum, Karl E., *Peace in Europe: East-West Relations, 1966-1969, and Prospects for European Settlement,* Oxford University Press, 1970.

Dziewanowski, M., *Poland in the 20th Century,* Colombia University Press, 1977.

Osborne, R. H., *East Central Europe,* Chatto & Windus, 1962.

Weigel, George, *Witness to Hope,* Cliff Street Book, 1999.

----*The Final Revolution: The Resistant Church and the Collapse of Communism,* Columbia University Press, 1992.

Articles in Periodicals and Books

Aspaturian, Vernon, "Eastern Europe in World Perspective," *Communism in Eastern Europe*, edited by Teresa Rakowska-Harmstone and Andrew Gyorgy, Indiana University Press, 1971.

Bland, C.L., "Trading with Eastern Europe," *Canada Commerce,* June/July, 1976.

King, Robert, "Bulgaria," *Communism in Eastern Europe. op. cit.*

Kirschbaum, Stanislav, "Twelve Months after Helsinki: A Debate Rages Over Détente," *International Perspective*, 1976, May/June.

Korbonski, Andrzej, "Poland," *Communism in Eastern Europe, op. cit.*

Kovrig, Bennett, "Hungary," *ibid.*

Kovacs, Imer, "The Establishment in Hungary," edited by Lyman H. Legters, *Eastern Europe, Transformation and Revolution, 1945-1990.*

Matas, David, "Helsinki Watch in Budapest," *International Perspective*, June/July, 1976.

McGuigan, Mark, "Atlantic Alliance Dedicated to the Preservation of Peace," *Statements and Speeches*, May, 17, 1982, DEA.

Page, Donald, "Hopes and Disappointing Realities," *Canadian-Soviet Relations. 1939-1980*, edited by Aloysius Balawyder, Mosaic Press, 1981.

Remington, Robin Allison, "Yugoslavia," *Communism in Eastern Europe, op. cit.*

Skilling, Gordon H., "Belgrade and Human Rights: Success or failure," *International Perspective*, Canadian National Library, Ottawa.

----"Canada and Eastern Europe," *Canadian Slavonic Papers*, vol.viii, 1966.

Svitak, Ivan, "Before the Occupation," *Communism in Eastern Europe, op.cit.*

Weslowski, Wlodzimiers, "Transition from Authoritarianism to Democracy," *Eastern Europe, op. cit.*

Weydental, Jan B., "The First Hundred Days of Walesa's Presidency," *ibid.*

For Reference Reading

Audy, Phyllis, *Tito: A Biography*, McGraw-Hill, 1970.

Bethell, Nicholas, *Gomulka, Pelican*, 1962.

Bothwell, Robert, John English, Ian Drummond, *Power, Politics, and Provincialism*, University of Toronto Press, 198.

Bromke, Adam, *Idealism and Realism*, Harvard University Press, 1967.

Brown, J.F., *Bulgaria Under Communist Rule*, Praeger, 1970.

Clarkson, Stephen In*dependent Foreign Policy for Canada*, University of Toronto Press, 1968.

Dubcek, Alexander, *Czechoslovakia's Blueprint for Freedom*, edited by Paul Echo, Washington, D.C.

Dziewanowski, M.K., *The Communist Party of Poland*, 2nd. Harvard University Press, 1976.

Eayrs, James, *In Defence of Canada*, University of Toronto Press, 1972-1980.

Fallenbuchl, Zbigniew, M, "The Polish Economy in 1970s"*East European Economies Post-Helsinki*. Washington, D.C.1977.

Fisher-Galati, Stephen, *The New Rumania: From People's Democracy to Socialist Republic*, MIT Press, 1967.

Hillmer, Norman, and Garth Stevenson, eds., *Foremost Nation: Canadian Foreign Policy and a Changing World, McClellan* & Stewart, 1977.

Holmes, J.W., *the Shaping of Peace: Canada and the Search for World Order 1943-1957*, 2 vols, University Toronto Press, 1979, 1982.

----*The Better Part of Valour and Canada: A Middle-Aged Power*, McClellan & Stewart, 1975.

Kecskemeti, Paul, *The Unexpected Revolution*, Stanford University Press, 1961.

King, Robert, *Minorities Under Communism*, Harvard University Press, 1973.

Korbanski, Andrzej, *Politics of Socialist Agriculture in Poland*, Colombia University Press, 1965.

Kusin, Vladimir, *The Intellectual Origins of the Prague Spring: The Development of Reformist Ideas in Czechoslovakia, 1956-1967*, Cambridge University Press, 1971.

Milenkovitch, Deborah D., *Plan and Market in Yugoslav Economic Thought*, Yale University Press, 1971.

Milosz, Czeslaw, *The Captive Mind*, Alfred A. Knopf, 1953.

Montias, John Michael, *Economic Development in Communist Rumania*, MIT Press, 1971.

Nagy, Imre, *On Communism: In Defense of the New Course*, London, 1957.

Oren, Nissan, *Bulgarian Communism: The Road to Power, 1933-1944*, Columbia University Press, 1971.

Reid, Escott, *Time of Fear and Hope*, McClellan & Stewart, 1977.

Roberts, Henry L., *Rumania: Political Problems of an Agrarian State*, Yale University Press, 1951.

Rubinstein, Alvin Z., *Yugoslavia and the Nonaligned World*, Princeton University Press, 1970.

Selucky, R., *Czechoslovakia: The Plan That Failed*, London 1970.

Skilling, H.Gordon, *Czechoslovakia's Interrupted Revolution*, Princeton University Press, 1976.

Thordarson, Bruce, *Trudeau and Foreign Policy*, University of Toronto Press, 1972.

Vali, Ferenc, *Rift and Revolt in Hungary*, Harvard University Press, 1961.

Whitaker, Reginald and Gary Marcuse, *Cold War Canada: The Making of a National Insecurity State*, University of Toronto Press, 1994.

Zacher, W.H (eds)., *Canadian Foreign Policy and the Law of the Sea,* University of British Columbia Press. 1977.

Zielinski, J.G., *Economic Reform in Polish Industry*, Oxford University Press, 1973.

Zinner, Paul E., *Revolution in Hungary*, Columbia University Press, 1962.

INDEX

L

M

N

O

P

R

S